HMS VANGUARD AT THE

the men, the ship, the battle

The Nelson Society©

ISBN No. 0-9510702-7-4

ADMIRAL LORD NELSON, K.B. and the VICTORY OF THE NILE
from a print published March 25th 1799 by George Riley, Old Bailey

Portrait from
L.F. Abbott Esq.

Embellishments drawn and engraved
by Piercey Roberts

The work was "zealously inscribed to J.J. Angerstein Esq. and the gentlemen who have so humanely, strenuously and successfully exerted themselves for the relief of the Widows and Orphans of those seamen who bravely fell on the above occasion."

ADMIRAL LORD NELSON K.B. and the VICTORY of the NILE

J.J. Angerstein
Mr Angerstein was of Russian extraction and came to England at the age of 15. He was introduced to Lloyd's and became a renowned broker and underwriter. He was well known for his philanthropic activities even before the formation of the Patriotic Fund, for he was chairman of five war funds, originating from Lloyd's, between 1794 and 1801. The dedication would therefore appear well warranted.

'The Salute' – Derek Gardner, VRD, R.S.M.A.
HMS Majestic (74) Source: The Missions to Seamen

HMS VANGUARD at the NILE –
the men, the ship, the battle

CONTENTS

Foreword by Mrs Anna Tribe, O.B.E., J.P. 6
List of Illustrations 7
Introduction 8
Acknowledgements 10

1 The Countdown to the Battle
   French And British Perspectives 11
2 The Official Report and Master's Log Entry –
   HMS Vanguard 45
3 *HMS Vanguard* 51
4 The Muster Book 52
5 The Aftermath 99
6 The Reception of the Victor 102
7 The Treasures on board *L'Orient* 110
8 Commemoratives/Contemporary Prints 111
9 Biographical Notes 120
   The Nelson Society 142
   List of Publications 144

FOREWORD

On the 7th December 1797 Nelson wrote to Captain Berry. "Our ship is at Chatham, a seventy four and she will be choicely manned, Ever yours most faithfully, Horatio Nelson."

Now, thanks to a great deal of work and research by the editorial team, we know the names of those who were so described. We have not only the muster lists but also other information about some of those on board, together with an account of the battle and various relevant letters and messages. We even have the letter of thanks that Nelson sent round to his captains or "Band of Brothers" as he called them, on the day after the battle. It is also most gratifying that the last codicil to Nelson's Will is quoted, one hopes confirming the story that Emma and the Queen of Naples facilitated arrangements for the British fleet to water and provision their ships at Syracuse in July 1798 on their way to Egypt.

Two interesting facts I have found from reading this. There were sixteen pressed men aboard, of which only nine were pressed for *Vanguard*. Also there were fifteen lads under 18 aboard ranging in age from Jon Bryant, aged 12, to Richard Martin who was 17. A record of this kind puts life into descriptions of *HMS Vanguard* and the Battle of the Nile. For it has to be remembered that although the battle might have been won without their Admiral it certainly would not have been won without these men. I am delighted that we now have a companion book to that previously written by Charles Addis in the same format describing those who fought on *HMS Victory* at Trafalgar. We must be very grateful to The Nelson Society for both publications.

Raglan, Gwent
May, 1998

Anna Tribe
Vice President, The Nelson Society

LIST OF ILLUSTRATIONS

Colour

	Page
The Battle of the Nile, G. Arnald (1763 – 1841) Front & Back cover (Front and Back covers)	
Attack at Sunset – Robert Dodd (1748 – 1815)	31
The Battle of the Nile – destruction of L'Orient Mather Brown (1761 – 1841)	32
Nelson wounded in cockpit of *Vanguard*	36
Captain Sir Edward Berry John Singleton Copley (1737 – 1815)	37

Black and White

	Page
Admiral Lord Nelson KB and the Victory of the Nile	2, 3
HMS Majestic (74) – Derek Gardner	4
François Paul Brueys d'Aigalliers, Comte de Brueys (1753 – 1798)	16
Routes of the English and French fleets	19
The dismasted *Vanguard* in tow of *Alexander*	25
Captains Ball and Saumarez	26
Plan of the Battle of the Nile (Source Unknown)	29
The Battle of the Nile 1 August 1798 – N. Pocock	33
HMS Superb (74) – Derek Gardner	35
The *Goliath* leading the British van – Charles Dixon	40
Nelson wounded in the battle of the Nile – Ernest Prater	41
Facsimile of Muster List entry	58, 59

	Page
Landsman	93
Sailors at Prayer led by Rev. S. Comyn	101
The reward of Courage, or Nelson Triumphant	102
Lady Hamilton welcoming the Victors – Robert Hollingford	104
Lady Hamilton – Schmidt	105
Hilt of Sword presented by Nelson's Captains	107
The Chelengk	108
Rudder support from *L'Orient*	110
The Alexander Davison Medals	111
The Naval General Service Medal	112
Pratt Ware jug	112
Contemporary Prints from the Dormers Collection:	
(i) Nelson's Defeat of the French	114
(ii) Portrait of Nelson presented to the Sultan of Turkey	115
(iii) The Glorious Battle of the Nile	116
(iv) Battle of the Nile	117
(v) Battle of the Nile showing explosion of *L'Orient*	118
(vi) Memorial to Nelson's victories	119
Lithograph of Tom Allen	122
Portrait of Greenwich Pensioners including Tom Allen	123
Sir Edward Berry, Pub. G. Riley 20 Jan 1799	128
Action between *Leander* and *Le Généreux* 18 August 1798	129
Revd. Stephen Comyn, B.A.	132
The arms of Revd. Stephen Comyn	133

INTRODUCTION

Graham Dean, as Archivist and Librarian of The Nelson Society, was instrumental in 1993 in arranging with family researcher, Joan Stollenwerk, for the Society to acquire copies of the Muster Lists of the vessels of Nelson's Squadron (thirteen 74's, the *Leander* (50) and *La Mutine* (brig)) which were engaged in the Battle of the Nile on 1 and 2 August 1798. The archives of the Society were thus enhanced and a most useful source for genealogical research established, and the lists are now in bound volumes and are being put on disk..

After the battle, the tribulations of some of the wounded being repatriated were made worse by subsequent events. The *Leander*, Captain Thompson, with Flag Captain Edward Berry carrying Nelson's dispatches on the battle, was forced to surrender to *Généreux* in an unequal engagement off Crete on 18 August and those who survived were to suffer exceedingly at the hands of the enemy and to become prisoners of war. Other wounded, homeward bound on the *Colussus*, were wrecked on the Scillies on December 7, 1798, but the exertions of Scillonians at least avoided loss of life. In this, the year of the Bi-centenary, *The Nelson Society* publishes a work which includes the Muster List of Nelson's ship *Vanguard*, as a tribute to the men who fought, were wounded and who died, in the virtual annihilation of the French Fleet under Vice Admiral de Brueys and which contributed to the frustration of Napoleon's ambitions of eastern conquest.

It would be ungenerous not to record that there were women who participated in the battle either as powder carriers or as nursing assistants and the Muster List of the *Goliath* records the mustering of four women, widows of men killed in battle, who were 'victualed at two-third allowance' in consideration of their assistance in dressing and attending to the wounded.

Much has been, and will continue to be, written on the battle but in this work the Editorial Team has concentrated not on the Battle but on the personnel and biographical information, where available, has been included. Nevertheless opportunity has been taken to include items of other topics relating to the Battle and the aftermath. Individual acts of heroism in the enemy fleet have been well recorded in poetry and elsewhere and their losses, as well as those of the Royal Navy, are remembered.

This publication develops the concept of the 1988 publication by *The Nelson Society* of *The Men who fought with NELSON in HMS VICTORY at TRAFALGAR*. It will, it is hoped, form a useful addition to the library of members and others interested in the Life and Times of Vice Admiral Lord Nelson. An invitation is extended to any reader with any information on any member of the crew of *Vanguard* or other ship engaged at the Nile to contact *The Nelson Society* so that the archive can be updated and extended.

Publication of this book was facilitated by generous acts of sponsorship by members of the Society to whom our sincere thanks are due.

July 1998   Derek Hayes, Chairman, *The Nelson Society*

A FRIGATE UNDER SAIL

ACKNOWLEDGEMENTS

Chandler, David *The Campaigns of Napoleon*
Howarth David and Stephen, *Nelson The Immortal Memory*, Dent & Sons Ltd
Lavery Brian, *Nelson's Navy* Conway Maritime Press Ltd
Masefield John, Methuen
Oman Carola, *Nelson*, Hodder and Stoughton
Oxford Companion to Ships and the Sea
Pocock Tom, *Horatio Nelson*, Bodley Head
Rodgers NAM, *Naval Records for Genealogists*, Public Record Office, Richmond
National Maritime Museum, London
Navy Records Society, *Great Sea Fights 1794-1805*
Dean Graham, Archivist
Nicolas, *The Dispatches and Letters of Lord Nelson*, Chatham Publishing reprint
Stollenwerk Joan, family researcher
Cross Anthony, Warwick Leadlay Gallery

The Editorial Team
The Nelson Society wishes to acknowledge with gratitude the efforts
of the members comprising the Editorial Team:
Eric Tushingham, John Morewood, Derek Hayes

•

And to thank David Shannon, Brian Tarpey,
Adrian Bridge, Sim Comfort, Ron Fiske
and other members who have contributed in so many ways.

CHAPTER 1

COUNTDOWN TO THE BATTLE

The Background

With the ease and comfort of a view from twenty decades, many features of the Battle of the Nile at Aboukir Bay near Alexandria, Egypt, on 1 & 2 August 1798, may be described as spectacular. There was the catastrophic loss of the Flagship *L'Orient* at the heart of the French fleet, whose detonation momentarily stilled the tumult of battle. Consider also the effect of a bejewelled 'Plume of Triumph', the *chelengk*, presented by the Sultan of Turkey to Nelson with thirteen rays representing the French vessels destroyed or taken. Turkey feared the further encroachment east of the French Army and thought a fatal blow had been delivered by the British fleet, but Napoleon's influence continued to stalk the land for many years hence. These spectacular features mask the continuing fear across Europe which, following the Revolution in France in 1789 and the death by guillotine of Louis XVl in 1793 did not subside until the final defeat of Napoleon at the Battle of Waterloo in 1815. Contemptuous of his opponents, Napoleon had described the modern Turkish army as a thing of little importance! As for Britain he said 'Should a victorious army ever enter London the world would be astonished at the trifling resistance that would be offered by the English' The threat of republicanism and the brutality which attended the rapacious French exploits across Europe, carried with it for the British uncomfortable echoes of their own civil war and the execution of Charles I. The destruction of the French fleet was a significant reverse, which continued to inhibit the territorial ambitions of Napoleon for years to come, not least by the example, and encouragement it gave to others.

Countdown to the Battle – the French perspective

France in 1798 was a self-confident power, which could afford to undertake overseas ventures. This had not been the case when she had gone to war in 1792. Known as the war of the First Coalition, France, in the throes of revolution, had been faced by a coalition of the powers of Spain, Holland, Austria, Prussia, Great Britain and Sardinia. Within five years, French forces administered knock out blows to their enemies removing the threat of invasion to France and extending her frontiers to the Rhine, the Alps and the Pyrenees with client republics in the Netherlands, Switzerland, Northern Italy and Rome and overseas possessions in the Ionian Isles. By 1797 only Austria and Great Britain still opposed her. Austria was forced to make peace as a result of the double threat posed by a French army crossing the Rhine and General Bonaparte's army being 75 miles from Vienna. This left Great Britain isolated. It was clearly in the French interest to force Britain to make peace for, as Bonaparte himself wrote, "Our Government must destroy the English monarch . . . Let us concert all our activity on the navy and destroy England. That done Europe is at our feet." The overseas venture being considered in 1798 was the invasion of Great Britain, not an expedition to the East.

Like most great historical events the change in the plan from an invasion of Great Britain to an invasion of Egypt was due to many factors. The most important was the relationship between France's newest military star Napoleon Bonaparte and the French Government. French politics of the period are complicated but basically there was an executive body known as the Directory comprising five directors and two elected chambers. 1797 had seen the Directors divided amongst themselves and the two elected chambers, following elections, wishing to pursue more pro royalist policies than the dominant Directors did. The leading three Directors called on dependable generals such as Bonaparte for support. In the *coup d'état* of Fructidor, which followed, the opposition to the Directors was crushed and the Directors became more beholden to Bonaparte than previously. War might have finished outside the French frontiers; there was however the question of what the unpopular Directors were to do with the successful generals and their armies who, given the peace, might themselves be tempted to seize power in France.

Of the generals the Directors had expected more of Hoche, Jourdan and Moreau than of Bonaparte and yet his achievements had been more than expected whilst the others had been disappointing. He had shown an ability to act independently of the French government compared to the other generals. In addition he also had more influence with the Directors as he had married a former mistress of one of them. All of this made him a danger and yet ensured him the top military appointment. On 26 October 1797 the Directors decided to form an army of England under Bonaparte's command comprising 120,000 men. Bonaparte returned from his Italian campaign to Paris in December and in January 1798 made a rapid tour of the proposed invasion embarkation points along the northern coast of France. His report was not what the Directors wanted but they could not ignore it. Bonaparte was convinced that the operation would be wholly impracticable until the French navy secured undisputed control of the Channel. Even if that was achieved the cost would be prohibitive, particularly as the Directory was faced with an inherited financial crisis which it was striving ably to resolve. With the invasion of England impractical, the possibility of a dangerous general being unemployed and new elections looming, the Directors needed to send Bonaparte as far from France as possible, but without causing a resumption of hostilities with the European powers, and with as little impact on French finances as possible. Given this scenario they were willing to accept any suggestion from Bonaparte. In his report Bonaparte offered them three suggestions: - peace with England, war against Hanover (of which George III was King) and, thirdly, a threat to England's rich commerce with India by way of an invasion of Egypt. The first two options were non-starters. The Directors could not make peace with such an ideologically opposed nation as England without defeating it first. An invasion of Hanover would provoke war on the continent. An invasion of Egypt was more suitable. It had, after all, been considered during the time of the French monarchy and there was still a belief in government circles in the need to expand the French colonies. All Napoleon had to do was sell the advantages of this concept in a pragmatic way and this is what he did, abetted by that master of intrigue, the French Foreign Minister Talleyrand.

  The concept was sold on the basis that an invasion of Egypt was an economical means of forcing England to make peace as well as compensating France for the loss of her West Indian possessions. There was the possibility of a lucrative domination of the ancient trade routes to Arabia and India and perhaps a canal could be dug through the Suez isthmus. Rapid and decisive action by France might also thwart British diplomatic endeavours to persuade the Ottoman empire to conclude an anti French alliance. A French army in Egypt could be presented as France trying to bring a recalcitrant province back under the Ottoman rule and therefore present the French Government favourably in Istanbul. The occupation of Egypt would offer an opportunity of re-establishing contact with anti British forces in India which had stopped following the British seizure of the Cape of Good Hope. Finally, why should not the most advanced and progressive society on Earth return some measure of prosperity to the people inhabiting one of the original cradles of civilisation?

How much of the above Bonaparte actually believed at the time we shall never know. He always rewrote accounts of his actions to portray himself in the most favourable light. We know he had spoken in the spring of 1797 of the need to secure Egypt and Malta as a way of making the Mediterranean a French controlled lake as well as hurting England. He was also fascinated by the lure of the East with its apparently limitless opportunities for military glory. Certainly, we know that he expected the expedition to be a short term affair. No more than six months was his first estimate. It was not yet time to overthrow the Directory and seize power but in six months the situation might be more favourable. The Directory approved his plan in March and on April 12, 1798 issued its orders. Bonaparte was instructed to capture Malta and Egypt, ordered to dislodge the English from the Orient, build a canal through the Isthmus of Suez, improve the situation of the local population and keep on good terms with the Sultan. There was no mention of an attack on India. The new republics in Switzerland and Rome would provide the finances and a diversionary attack prepared against Ireland. At the end of six months Bonaparte would return to France and take command of the postponed invasion of England.

Once the decision was made the whole expedition was prepared in ten weeks (five weeks from the formal issuing of the orders!). The organisation was complicated: -

- There were to be five embarkation ports (Toulon, Marseilles, Genoa, Ajaccio and Civita Vechia).
- Nearly 37,500 troops (infantry, cavalry and artillerymen) were to be embarked along with 500 civilians (167 noted men of letters and science who were to study Egypt).
- 60 field and 40 siege guns were to be embarked along with hard rations for 100 days, fresh water for 40 days and a total of 1,200 horses.

- The troops and civilians were to be transported in a convoy of some 400 transports protected by a fleet of thirteen ships of the line and a similar number of frigates.
- Leading lights of the French navy were to serve in the expedition. Some, for example, Emeriau and du Petit Thouars had seen service during the American War. Commodore Ganteaume, a future Admiral and commander at Brest, was the Chief of Staff. Rear Admiral Decres, a future Minister of Marine, commanded the convoy. Rear Admiral Blanquet du Chayla, a consummate seaman, with much experience of fighting the British, commanded part of the fleet, and Rear Admiral Villeneuve another part. Command of the fleet was entrusted to the most recent hero of the French navy, de Brueys, instead of the expected commander Blanquet du Chayla.

Francois Paul Brueys d'Aigalliers, Comte de Brueys (1753-1798)
De Brueys was 45 years old and had joined the French navy as a volunteer at the age of 13. In the last few years he had experienced rapid promotion. In 1796 he had been promoted Rear Admiral and had reached Napoleon's notice by taking possession of the Ionian Islands and capturing a larger force of Venetian ships lying at Corfu. He was promoted to the rank of Vice Admiral for the expedition and had as his flagship the 120 gun *L'Orient*. This was his largest command to date and in a letter of his to the Minister of Marine in Paris we can perhaps detect a lack of confidence. "Our crews are very weak both in numbers and the quality of the men: our ships are, in general, ill-armed, and I think that it requires considerable courage to undertake the command of ships so ill fitted." Although the strength of the fleet was impressive on paper it is estimated that the fleet was 2,000 sailors under strength and "composed of men picked up at hazard and almost at the moment of sailing." To add to de Brueys' problems, although supposedly in charge of the naval side of the operation, he took orders from Bonaparte who, with his staff, installed himself on the flagship.

Francois Paul Brueys d'Aigalliers, Comte de Brueys (1753-1798)
From the drawing by A. Maurin, National Maritime Museum, London.

16

The French Sail

Despite these problems everything went well. The various rendezvous were achieved allowing the convoy to increase in numbers. The only difficulty experienced was when General Desaix failed to make his rendezvous and the convoy lost three days although the final link-up was achieved at Malta. Malta was taken against only nominal opposition and General Vaubois and 4,000 men landed to garrison Valetta. De Brueys, no doubt in consultation with Bonaparte, set a course for Crete in order to deceive Nelson and then south to Egypt. On the night of June 22-23 the different courses of the two fleets crossed but the British were unaware of the enemy's proximity although some of the French sailors heard alien ships' bells. That the French fleet, slowed down by its large convoy, had managed to avoid Nelson was unbelievably lucky and on 1 July the French reached Alexandria. The landings took place at a village near Alexandria called Marabout. De Brueys was over ruled by Bonaparte and the landings, poorly co-ordinated, went on through the night resulting in the landing boats being overturned and men drowned. Alexandria was seized and by 10 July all the French troops had begun to advance into the interior. Admiral de Brueys had achieved all his objectives but he was to remain in Aboukir Bay for another three weeks.

TIMETABLE OF THE FRENCH FLEET

19th May 1798	Embarkation at Marseilles and Toulon of General Bonaparte Staff and escort: 500, Civilian contingent: 500, troops commanded by Generals Kleber, Bon and Reynier: 16,000. Convoy escorted by 13 ships of the line and 13 frigates.
21st May 1798	Convoy rendezvous with subsidiary convoy from Genoa under Command of D'Hilliers and Murat. Infantry and cavalry: 7,100.
23rd May 1798	Convoy rendezvous off Sardinia with subsidiary convoy from Ajaccio under command of General Vaubois. Troops: 4,500
23rd – 26th May	Convoy waits in vain for another subsidiary convoy commanded by General Desaix. Troops 8,200
26th May 1798	Desaix leaves Civita Vecchia and sails direct for Malta
6th June 1798	Desaix arrives at Malta
9th June 1798	Convoy arrives at Malta and joins with Desaix
10-12th June	French landings on Malta
19th June 1798	Convoy leaves Malta
22-23rd June	(Night) Convoy nearly runs into Nelson's fleet
26th June 1798	French fleet off Crete
27th June 1798	French fleet warned of Nelson's proximity by frigate
1-3rd July 1798	Main landing

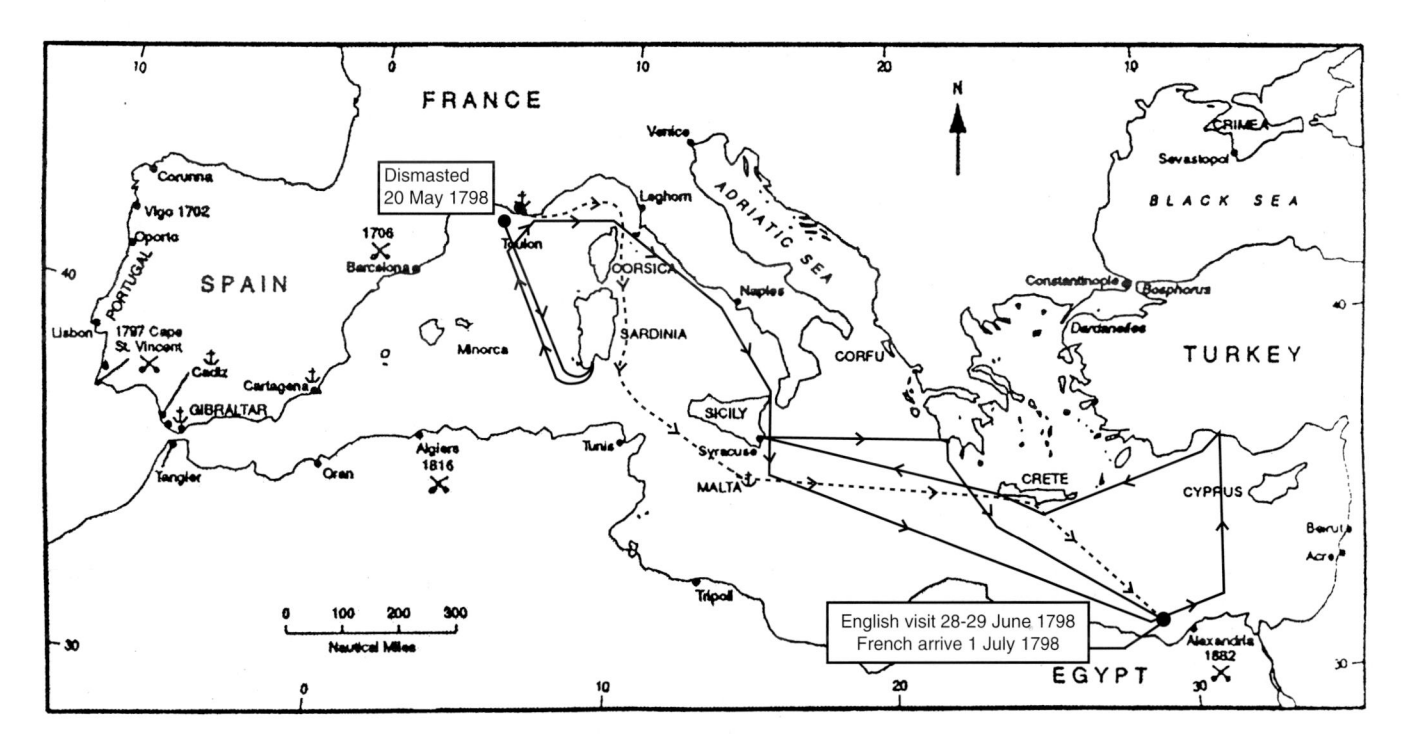

THE MEDITERRANEAN

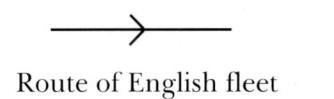

19

The French Fleet at Aboukir
Bonaparte subsequently blamed de Brueys for the disaster in terms of both the tactical disposition and the very fact that the French fleet should have been at sea and not moored at Aboukir at all. Contemporary correspondence however reveals that the French fleet stayed at anchor on the direct orders of Bonaparte himself. The navy had wanted to sail for Corfu to pick up further ships of the line. Bonaparte however probably wanted the fleet to protect the transports in Alexandria harbour from attack.

As there were doubts that the whole French fleet could safely enter Alexandria harbour the best option was to be positioned in Aboukir Bay - 23 miles east. In addition stores still needed to be unloaded, wells were being dug, and this explains why many of the sailors were ashore when Nelson attacked, as does the fact that Bonaparte had ordered the sailors to fulfil quasi military duties. Given this, what was crucial was for the fleet to be positioned in a way which would repel attack.

On first taking anchorage on 4 July, de Brueys held a council of flag officers and captains and, with the exception of Blanquet, all had agreed that in case of attack the fleet should engage at anchor and not under sail. Use was to be made of the geography of the bay. The western end of the semi circular bay was marked by Aboukir Point and Aboukir Island and shoals to seaward of it, with a connecting line of rocks and shoals narrowing the mouth of the bay. The island and the point were fortified. De Brueys' ships of the line were moored in a slightly bent line stretching south from the shallows just inside the island. Four frigates were anchored at intervals inside the line and the smaller ships in shallow water.

The thirteen French ships of the line were anchored with *L'Orient* in the middle of the line and a concentration of powerful 80 gun ships at the rear where de Brueys expected the attack to come. Inexcusably de Brueys did not have his frigates at sea to warn him of Nelson's approach. Also the leading French ship *Le Guerrier* had not anchored close enough to the shoals and the ships were not close enough to give supporting fire to each other. Nevertheless, to an admiral other than Nelson the prospect of attack might have proved daunting. De Brueys was certainly happy with his position. On 13 July he wrote to Bonaparte: "I have been taking up a strong position in case I am compelled to fight at anchor". The stage was now set for the battle.

The British Perspective

In 1797 reports were circulating of a gathering of a French fleet and troops, likely to disembark from Toulon, whose destination could be Ireland, the West Indies, Naples, Sicily or Portugal. On 30 April Lord Spencer, in Whitehall, wrote, "the appearance of a British squadron in the Mediterranean is a condition on which the fate of Europe may at this moment be stated to depend".

Nelson

Following the amputation of part of his arm at Santa Cruz, Nelson spent seven uncomfortable months in England in 1797. Convalescing but also socialising, much to the pleasure of his wife Fanny née Nisbet, who daily dressed his wound and attended to his food until he mastered the task of cutting and eating with one hand. At that time in an unusual period of domesticity they agreed to purchase 'Roundwood' a substantial house of eleven rooms set in fifty acres of ground outside Ipswich though Nelson was never to reside there. Interestingly, one of the witnesses to the signing of the agreement to the purchase for £2000 was Captain Berry. As Nelson recovered his health there were delays in fitting his flagship the new *Foudroyant* and he was given the ten-year-old seventy-four gun *Vanguard*. Edward Berry took responsibility as Captain for fitting her out and working up the ship's company for sea. On 29 March, 1798, Nelson embarked in the roads off St Helens on the easterly tip of the Isle of Wight. Detained by contrary winds Nelson was also discomforted by failures in the packing of his luggage about which he complained with gusto to his wife. Finally on 10 April 1798 the wind blew enabling the *Vanguard* and convoy to shed the constraints of anchor for Lisbon. In a private letter his Commander-in-Chief, Lord St Vincent wrote on 11 May 1798: " . . . You, and only you, can command the important service in contemplation; therefore make the best of your way down to me . . . You shall also have some choice Fellows of the in-shore Squadron."

The mouth of the Tagus offered a convenient base for the continuing blockade of Cadiz and Nelson received a warm welcome from St.Vincent, Commander-in-Chief of the British Fleet.

Reports had been reaching London through the spring that a major expeditionary force, together with its fleet of transports and escorting fleet of warships, was preparing to leave Toulon and the ports of that coast, including Marseilles and Genoa. It was known Napoleon was in command but his destination was a mystery. He could be bound for any country bordering the Mediterranean - including the now neutral Kingdom of the Two Sicilies - or preparing to attack Portugal or by breaking out into the Atlantic, for a descent upon Lisbon, or even upon Ireland to encourage a revolt against the British. Initially designated for reconnaissance with three sail-of-the-line and three frigates; under instruction from the Admiralty, Rear Admiral Sir Horatio Nelson, KB. was finally placed in charge of a squadron with thirteen 74's, one 50 gun sail of the line, and three frigates, it would be his task to find the French.

Edward Berry

Nelson described the captain of the *Vanguard*, Edward Berry, as having the countenance of a poet and the manner of an efficient officer and gentleman. At the Battle of St. Vincent on 14 February, 1797, Berry, was travelling as a passenger in the *Captain* (having recently been promoted). He was the first man to board the *San Nicolas*, an enemy 80 gun ship-of-the-line, following Nelson's audacious initiative in turning out of line to confront the Spanish fleet. When Nelson gained the quarterdeck of the enemy vessel he found Berry already in possession of the poop, engaged in hauling down the Spanish ensign. In the crossing to the San Josef it was Berry who assisted Nelson into the main chains, and a firm friendship was established for the remainder of their careers together.

On 25 September, 1797, Nelson attended St. James's Palace following the loss of part of his arm earlier in the year during the ill-fated assault on Santa Cruz. On meeting King George, the monarch exclaimed, 'You have lost your right arm!' and Nelson responded, 'But not my right hand, as I have the honour of presenting Captain Berry'.

A measure of the regard between the men may be gathered by the tone of Nelson's letter of 28 November 1797 to Berry on the occasion of his engagement. 'Any event which has the prospect of adding to your felicity cannot but afford me pleasure'. Events moved fast and on 8 December 1797 he was to write,

'To Captain Berry RN SECRET My dear Sir, If you mean to marry. I would recommend your doing it speedily, or the to be Mrs Berry will have very little of your company: for I am well, and you may be expected to be called for every hour. We shall probably be at sea before the *Foudroyant* is launched. Our ship is at Chatham, a Seventy-four, and she will be choicely manned. Ever yours most faithfully, Horatio Nelson'

The Chase

Early in 1798 Napoleon had visited the Channel ports of France and lent weight to the rumours of an invasion of England. It was also rumoured there would be an expedition to the East, and the capture of a French corvette, on 17 May 1798, confirmed that an armada was being fitted out in Toulon consisting of 3,000 transports, 50 warships, and 40,000 troops. If Egypt was the target, it would be likely to affect England's trade links, making it imperative that the British fleet re-enter the Mediterranean. The Commander-in-Chief Earl St. Vincent, blockading off Cadiz, showed his pleasure at the arrival of Nelson writing, 'The arrival of Admiral Nelson has given me new life'.

Nelson relished the task of seeking the French Fleet but the search had an uncertain start when on 20 May 1798 the *Vanguard* was partially dismasted in heavy weather killing two of her crew and was only saved by the exertions of Captain Ball and the crew of the *Alexander* and Captian James Saumarez of the *Orion*. A consequence of the severe storm was that Nelson lost the use of his frigates which ran for shelter and repair at Gibraltar. At the same time, just a few miles away and unknown to Nelson, the French fleet was leaving from Toulon. As the shipwrights toiled to repair the *Vanguard*, on the Isle of Sardinia, Nelson confided in a letter to his wife that the storm was a check on his vanity.

Within a few days repairs were effected and Nelson was so impressed he wrote a letter to his Commander in Chief commending by name Mr Morrison the carpenter of the *Alexander*. On the 7 June 1798 the squadron of seventy-four gun ships of the line was split into two columns, and without frigates, the search began.

The Order of Battle and Sailing was conveyed to the captains by the *Leander* of 50 guns

Starboard	Men	Captain	**Larboard**	Men	Captain
Culloden	590	Troubridge	Defence	590	Peyton
Theseus	590	Miller	Zealous	590	Hood
Alexander	590	Ball	Orion	590	Saumarez
Vanguard	595	Berry	Goliath	590	Foley
Minotaur	640	Louis	Majestic	590	Westcott
Swiftsure	590	Hallowell	Bellerophon	590	Darby
Audacious	590	Gould			

As Nelson sailed off the coast of Italy, calling at Naples, the French fleet made slower progress off the east coast of Corsica and Sardinia, and indeed, on one evening during the voyage, heard the sound of a signal gun from

The dismasted "Vanguard" in tow of "Alexander", Captain Alexander Ball
National Maritime Museum, London.

Rear-Admiral Sir Alexander John Ball
(1757 – 1809)

Captain of *Alexander*, salvor of *Vanguard*, participated fully in the battle and afterwards sent by Nelson to blockade and take Malta. Later appointed Governor of Malta and died there in 1809 and is remembered by a statue in picturesque gardens and in the naming of a bastion.

Admiral Lord James Saumarez
(1757 – 1836)

In command of *Orion* and assisted in the repair of the dismasted *Vanguard*. Second in command to Nelson, fought with distinction in the battle and was afterwards ordered by Nelson to Gibraltar with the prizes and thereafter continued a distinguished naval career.

the British squadron. In his letters Nelson lamented, 'My distress from want of frigates is extreme'. As the French occupied and garrisoned Malta, the British squadron eagerly pushed south through the Straits of Messina, off the toe of Italy, directly to Alexandria. They arrived there on the 28 June 1798 to find only Turkish vessels. In his eagerness, and without the 'eyes' of the frigates he so craved, Nelson had arrived too soon and promptly left on the 29 June, to continue the search to the North, just as the French were approaching from the West. The French landed at Marabout near Alexandria on the 1 July., Napoleon took Alexandria on the 2 July and Cairo on the 24 July, 1798. As the British replenished their water and provisions in Syracuse under arrangements facilitated by Lady Hamilton with the Queen of Naples (and referred to in the 'last' codicil to Nelson's will) he received confirmation of the path of the French and determined, with his captains, to return to Alexandria.

As he prepared to leave, Nelson wrote a short acknowledgement:–
TO SIR WILLIAM AND LADY HAMILTON
22 July, 1798

My dear Friends,
Thanks to your exertions, we have victualled and watered: and surely watering at the Fountain of Arethusa, we must have victory. We shall sail with the first breeze, and be assured I will return, either crowned with laurel, or covered with cypress."

By this time Napoleon had already seized Alexandria and was preparing to march for Cairo and oust the Mameluke Army. Throughout the voyage back to Alexandria, whenever the weather and circumstances permitted, Nelson had his captains on board the *Vanguard* where he would develop his ideas of the different and best methods of attack, whatever the position might be day or night. Every captain was thoroughly acquainted with the position their commander would adopt upon sighting the enemy, minimising the requirement for signalling detailed instructions. Gun crews were practised daily to sharpen their skills in handling the armaments. On the afternoon of 1 August 1798, a masthead lookout on the *Zealous* sighted the enemy in Aboukir Bay off the western mouth of the Nile. Thirteen French ships-of-the-line were anchored in a curve running to the northwest and guns had been landed on an island near the lead ship to seek to deter an assault. Although late in the day Nelson signalled 'Prepare for Battle' Nelson's plan was to concentrate the attack on the van and centre. Ships were to anchor by the stern, with ropes attached to their anchor cables to keep them at the right angle for firing most effectively. And having destroyed one of the enemy's ships from that position, they would, if need be, move down the line to the next sitting stationary target. As dusk was approaching distinctive lights were to be shown at their mizzenmasts to identify them as British ships, an obviously practical precaution given the failing light. Captains were also required to keep measuring the depth as they entered the bay to avoid grounding. As the British line gradually took shape Nelson, with some satisfaction, ordered dinner to be served.

The Battle

The Commander of the French fleet did not survive the Battle and may have felt confident in his position, with considerable advantage in firepower. The *L'Orient* of 120 guns was at the heart of the line of 13 ships, which included three sail-of-the-line of 80 guns, and from this stable position they were able to deliver a substantial response to any assault. However the British squadron of thirteen 74 gun ships and one of 50 guns led by Nelson and his 'Band of Brothers' were formidable opponents, having spent frustrating weeks blockading and then searching across many hundreds of miles of a bare ocean. Nelson dreamed of glory and his sailors of prizes but they were all fired by a determination to destroy the French. At about 6.30pm 1 August 1798 Captain Foley in the *Goliath* led the line and as he approached he spotted the opportunity to ease through the shallows on the landward side, which he did with care and skill, to place himself against his enemy. He sent a broadside into the first ship the *Le Guerrier* before anchoring against the inside of the *Le Conquérant*, which was the second French ship in the van. His initiative was followed by Hood in the *Zealous*, Gould in the *Audacious*, Miller in the *Theseus*, and Sir James Saumarez, Nelson's second-in-command, in the *Orion*. The van could then be attacked on two sides and was crushed before any support could be rallied.

The *Vanguard* anchored first on the outer side of the French line and was opposed within half pistol-shot to the *Spartiate*, the third in the French line. In standing in, the leading ships were unavoidably obliged to receive into their bows the whole fire of the broadsides of the French until they could take their respective stations.

PLAN OF THE BATTLE OF THE NILE.

August 1st, 1798.

The British Ships approaching the enemy's line are represented thus ▬ with the Capitals A B C &c. referring to their names: and the point of view is from the S. E. part of the Bay.—British ships at their respective stations in the attack are represented thus ◁ and the dotted lines shew their respective tracks. A Goliath ; B Zealous ; C Orion ; D Audacious ; E Theseus ; F Vanguard ; G Minotaur ; H Bellerophon ; I Defence ; K Majestic ; L Alexander ; M Swiftsure ; of 74 guns each. N Leander, 50 guns ; O Culloden, 74 guns ; P Mutine, 14 guns.

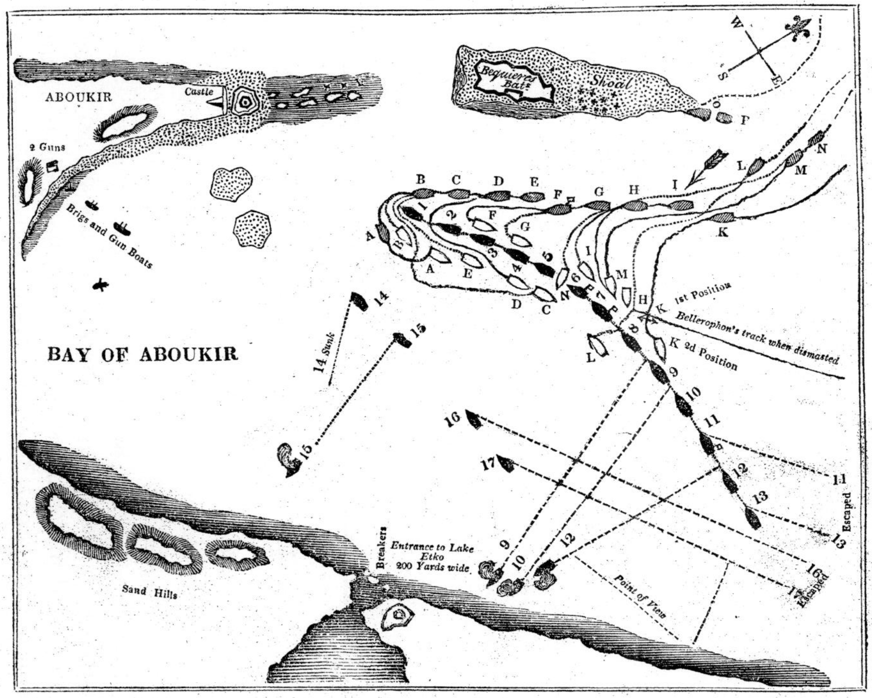

The French Line of Battle Ships are represented thus ▬ 1 Le Guerrier, 74 guns, taken and afterwards burnt as unserviceable ; 2 Le Conquerant, 74 guns, taken ; 3 Le Spartiate, 74 guns, taken ; 4 L'Aquilon, 74 guns, taken ; 5 Le Peuple Souverain, 74 guns, taken ; 6 Le Franklin, 80 guns, taken ; 7 L'Orient, 120 guns, burnt ; 8 Le Tonnant, 80 guns, taken ; 9 Le Heureux, 74 guns, taken and afterwards burnt ; 10 Le Timoleon, 74 guns, burnt ; 11 Le Guillaume Tell, 80 guns, escaped ; 12 Le Mercure, 74 guns, taken and afterwards burnt ; 13 Le Généreux, 74 guns, escaped.—Frigates, 14 La Sérieuse, 36 guns, sunk ; 15 L'Artemise, 40 guns, burnt ; 16 La Diane, 44 guns, escaped ; 17 La Justice, 44 guns, escaped. The Alert, Infanta, and Castor, mortar vessels, of 18 guns each, ran in shore under the castle of Aboukir.

Source unknown (watermarked 1812)
Reproduced in *The Nelson Dispatch* Vol.1 Part 3, July 1982.

Throughout the approach of the English ships-of-the-line the French remained steady, no colours being hoisted or a gun being fired until the English van was within half gun shots. The English sailors were busy at this time, aloft, furling sails, and on deck, hauling braces and preparing to cast anchor. As *Vanguard* opened fire the following ships passed close by and took their positions opposed to the French line. The *Leander* of 50 guns raked *Le Franklin* and shot from the broadside carried to strike *L'Orient*.

As planned the *Defence, Minotaur, Bellerophon, Majestic, Swiftsure, Alexander*, and *Leander* followed and took position against targets in the French line. Much to the disgust of Captain Troubridge the *Culloden* was the only ship-of-the-line not to engage the enemy having grounded on the shoals in the approach to the battle.

Within half an hour of the commencement of firing, it was dark, but by that time *Le Guerrier, Le Conquerant* and *Le Spartiate* were dismasted. By half past eight in the evening, *L'Aquilon* and *Le Souverain Peuple* were taken. Captain Berry sent Lieutenant Galwey with a party of Marines to take possession of *Le Spartiate* and he returned with the French captain's sword.

Nelson on the *Vanguard*, which came under heavy fire early in the action, was hit in the head by a piece of iron. Blood streamed down on his good eye at such a rate that he thought it must be the end and he was led below where the surgeon was attending the injured.

As Doctor Jefferson became aware of his presence he moved to attend to the Admiral but Nelson said, "No. I will wait my turn with my brave fellows." Nelson was sure death was near, called for the chaplain, and saw to it that messages were prepared for Lady Nelson, and for Captain Louis of the *Minotaur* to thank him for the support his vessel had given the flagship. In fact Nelson's wound, though messy, was not dangerous and, after being stitched up by the surgeon, he returned to the upper deck and saw the last moments of the *L'Orient*. The battle was furious but the initiative

Figurehead and stern ornaments of "The Bellerophon"

"The Bellerophon", disabled, drops out of action

Attack at Sunset – Robert Dodd.

Sim Comfort Collection

The Battle of the Nile – destruction of L'Orient. Mather Brown (1761-1831). National Maritime Museum, London.

The unfinished scene depicted is the falling of the mast of *La Spartiate* and reflects the artist's concern for the plight of the sailors as opposed to ships. The rescue of enemies shows the triumph of courage and humanity.

THE BATTLE OF THE NILE, 1ST AUGUST 1798 N. Pocock

The position of L'Orient is clearly identified by the artist

by the British was never lost, though exhaustion slowed the action during the course of the evening. At about 10 o'clock the *L'Orient* was seen to be on fire, largely as a result of the bravery and skill of three ships including the *Bellerophon* and her crew who suffered grievously in the effort. As some French sailors were ashore creating wells and replenishing stores, the opportunity had been taken for routine maintenance on the *L'Orient* and paint, tar and barrels of pitch left on deck, as well as inflammable incendiaries, accelerated the demise of the 120 gun flagship. After blazing for some time the *L'Orient* blew up with a detonation heard thirteen miles away in Alexandria by French troops. Most of her company, were killed. Also believed lost was treasure looted by Napoleon from Malta. A midshipman on the *Swiftsure* heard from survivors of the bravery of de Brueys, who having been wounded in the head, arm, and then almost cut in two, was seated, with tourniquets on the stumps of his legs, in an armchair facing his enemies until he died on his quarterdeck.

Nelson ordered the *Vanguard's* only undamaged boat to pick up some of *L'Orient's* crew he could see struggling in the water. Before the battle was over he sent for his secretary to begin a dispatch but neither the secretary nor the chaplain was able to write. Nelson himself, with guns thundering and the night sky bright with explosions, sat down and wrote to Lord St. Vincent.

"My Lord, Almighty God has blessed His Majesty's Arms in the late Battle by a great Victory over the Fleet of the Enemy, who I attacked at sunset on the 1st August, off the mouth of the Nile." He went on to commend his officers and men, lamenting the loss of Captain Westcott of the *Majestic* who had been hit in the throat by a musket ball. Fighting continued according to Poussielgue, Bonaparte's Controller General of Finances until 3 o'clock in the morning. It then "ceased almost until 5 o'clock: then it continued with as much fury as ever." Another French ship of the line *Le Timoleon* was set on fire by her crew and blew up. Poussielgue reported, "Firing continued until about 2 o'clock in the afternoon and then we saw two of the line and two frigates under a press of sail on a wind, standing towards the eastward: we make out that all were under French colours. No other ships made any movement and firing ceased entirely." The Battle of the Nile was over. The area was a scene of devastation about which Nelson said, "Victory is not a name strong enough for such a scene." Of the thirteen French ships of the line and the four frigates, which had opposed him, all but four were smoking hulks, sunk, held as prizes or helplessly grounded. Of the four ships that escaped, two were mere frigates. The survivors were led away by Rear

Admiral Villeneuve, unpursued, since no British ship was in a condition to chase them, though Miller in the *Theseus*, the least damaged, pursued them until recalled by signal. Of the *Vanguard* officers Captain William Faddy, Marines and Midshipmen Thomas Seymour and John G Taylor were killed; Lieutenant Nathaniel Vassal and John M. Adye, John Campbell, Admiral's Secretary, Boatswain Michael Austin and Midshipmen John Weatherstone and George Antrim were injured.

The 74-gun ship HMS Superb
Derek Gardner, V.R.D, R.S.M.A. Source: The Missions to Seamen

His head bandaged to staunch the flow of blood from a shrapnel wound, Admiral Nelson orders the ship's surgeon to treat more seriously wounded crewmen first.

National Maritime Museum, London

Captain Sir Edward Berry   John Singleton Copley (1737-1815)
National Maritime Museum, London.

Anchoring by the stern
The ships of Nelson's Squadron were trained and prepared to anchor by the stern if required and this was effected at the battle. The actual mechanics were discussed in the columns of *The Nelson Dispatch* (Vol. 5 Parts 2,3 and 4).

The usual method of anchoring by the stern was to lead the cable through a stern port and then attach it to the sheet anchor. The sheet anchor was as large as the main or bower anchors and usually reserved for emergencies. Due to its weight it would have been difficult and time-consuming to carry the anchor to the stern by boat. In any event there was no cathead or other fixture at the stern stout enough to raise or lower an anchor and if there had been there was the danger of the flukes damaging the stern windows or quarter galleries. Where stern davits were fitted these were for raising and lowering boats and although they were similar to the anchor davits located at the bow, the anchor davits only supported a part of the weight of the anchor as it was moved from the vertical to the horizontal. The main weight of the anchor fell upon the cathead. Therefore the usual method of anchoring by the stern was to drop the anchor from the bow. In the Naval Battles of Great Britian, published in 1828, Charles Ekins gives a detailed account of the *Goliath* performing this manoeuvre at the Battle of the Nile.

> "All sail was now taken in, except the mizen-topsail, which was thrown aback, and when thus very slowly passing the bow of the *Guerrier*, within a ship's length, the action commenced on our side by a most dreadfully destructive raking fire. The anchor was at the same time dropped from the bow, the cable being in at the stern port; but having no after bitts, when the ship swung stern to the wind, and the sails began to fly loose from the running rigging being out, it became difficult to stopper the cable. It kept surging for some minutes, and at last carried all away, and ran out to the clinch, placing the *Goliath* on the quarter of the second, and on the bow of the third ship of the French line, so as to engage both."

Goliath, 74 guns, had been built at Deptford and launched in 1781, and was finally broken up in 1815. Under Captain Foley the ship was turned shorewards to pass between the *Guerrier* and the shore. The delay in the anchor taking the way off the ship meant that she finally stopped in a position opposite the second and third vessels of the French line with her originally intended position being taken by *Zealous*.

To stopper the cable is to temporarily hold the cable so that the inboard end can be handled. Cdr. Geoff Hunt's view is that in the case of the *Goliath* the stopper failed and the cable surged out.

To clinch is the method of fastening large ropes to heavy objects by a half hitch with the end stopped back on its own part by seizing.

In the absence of after bitts on the *Goliath*, Peter Goodwin of *Victory* says the cable would normally have been led through to the forward bitts. Even so, the mizzen mast would have been strong enough for the purpose, assuming the cable was checked with a check stopper and not allowed to snatch at the mast. All this was, of course, happening when the ship was in action and it reflects the degree of training and discipline that permitted simultaneous difficult navigational and fighting activities. The moment that *Goliath* crossed the bows of *Guerrier* is depicted in the picture by Charles Dixon.

The Goliath, leading the British van, crossing the bows of the Guerrier C. Dixon

Nelson wounded in the Battle of the Nile. *Ernest Prater*

The immediacy of electronic communications in 1998 would have astounded sailors at the Nile and been viewed with envy by the politicians who had months to wait before the dispatches arrived with the momentous news from the Mediterranean. We have the benefit of being able to read their letters as they passed information and formal reports, and can only marvel at their courage and grace under testing circumstances. The mutual respect and regard they had for each other shines across the centuries through the correspondence.

TO THE CAPTAINS OF THE SHIPS OF THE SQUADRON

Vanguard, of the Mouth of the Nile 2 August, 1798

"The Admiral most heartily congratulates the Captains, Officers, Seamen and Marines of the Squadron he has the honour to Command, on the event of the late Action; and he desires they will accept his sincere and cordial Thanks for their gallant behaviour in the glorious Battle...HORATIO NELSON"

TO SIR HORATIO NELSON, K.B.

"*Audacious*, 1 August, 1798

"I have the satisfaction to tell you the French Ship, Le Conquerant has struck to the Audacious and I have her in possession. The slaughter on board her is dreadful: her Captain is dying. We have but one killed, but a great many wounded. Our fore and mainmast are wounded, but I hope not very bad. They tell me the foremast is the worst. I give you joy. This is a glorious victory. I am, with the utmost respect, yours in haste.

D. Gould."

"From Captain Foley of the *Goliath*   2 August, 1798

After congratulating you on the most signal Victory possible to be gained at sea, I take leave to inquire after your wound which I trust will not be of serious consequence. I should not have waited the message you sent to me to give assistance to the Theseus could I have secured my mainmast sooner. The dread of losing it and the appearance of so little defence on the side of the Enemy this morning induced me to be so late in heaving my anchor. The rigging more than the mast is the damaged part. I shall send a boat to sound towards the Ships which keep French colours up. As soon as I can get the soundings I will endeavour to get nearer them. As far as I can at present collect, the Killed on board the *Goliath* are seventeen with thirty-three wounded. I have the honour to be, dear Sir, your faithful and obedient Servant. Th. FOLEY"

Two letters from Captain Berry (Nelson's Flag-Captain) to Captain Miller of the *Theseus*

My dear Miller   *Vanguard*, 2nd August

"There is but one heart and one soul in this glorious Victory; your very handsome conduct we saw, and felt; the Admiral is conscious of your doing right, and leaves it to you to order. He congratulates and thanks you, - hopes your wounds are of no consequence, as you say; Sir Horatio, I believe, to be out of danger, though his wound is in the head, and he has been sick. Send a letter or a word to me for your wife as I may soon be off. God bless you, my dear friend. Ever yours most truly. E.BERRY"

My dear Miller   *Vanguard*, 3 August.

"I am desired by Sir Horatio to say, you are to take the whole charge of the dismasted Prize you are near - He knows she is badly off for ground tackling, and knows you will do all you can. He is now more easy than he was this morning, the rage being over. Your getting under weigh pleased him much. You know I am ever yours most truly, E.BERRY"

Establishment of the Egyptian Club

On the 3 August the Captains of the Squadron met on board the *Orion* under Captain Sir James Saumarez the senior captain and second in command in the Battle and formed a resolution testifying their admiration of their Chief: "... request (Rear-Admiral Sir Horatio Nelson K.B.) his acceptance of a Sword; and, as a further proof of their esteem and regard, hope that he will permit his Portrait to be taken, and hung up in the Room belonging to the Egyptian Club, now established in commemoration of that glorious day."
To which resolution they all added their signatures.

The following letters from Nelson also show the skills of diplomacy required in such circumstances being remote from the Admiralty and even his Commander in Chief.

TO THE RIGHT HONOURABLE SIR WILLIAM HAMILTON, K.B.

Vanguard, Mouth of the Nile, 8 August, 1798

"My Dear Sir

Almighty God has made me the happy instrument in destroy the Enemy's Fleet, which I hope will be a blessing to Europe. You will have the goodness to communicate this happy event to all the Courts in Italy,..."

TO HIS EXCELLENCY THE GOVERNOR OF BOMBAY

Vanguard, Mouth of the Nile, 9 August, 1798

"Sir

Although I hope the Consuls who are, or ought to be resident in Egypt, have sent you an express of the situation of affairs here, yet, as I know Mr Baldwin has some months left Alexandria, it is possible you may not be regularly informed. I shall, therefore, relate to you, briefly, that a French Army of 40,000 men in 300 transports, with 13 Sail of the Line, 11 Frigates, Bomb Vessels, Gunboats, &c. arrived at Alexandria on the 1 July". The letter continued to describe the outcome of the fleet battle and Nelson's intention to inhibit any further expansion east by Bonaparte, who Nelson believed was suffering from lack of stores and artillery as a result of intercepted dispatches.

CHAPTER 2

THE OFFICIAL REPORT

TO ADMIRAL THE EARL OF ST. VINCENT, K.B., COMMANDER-IN-CHIEF.
[From the "Letter-book" and "London Gazette Extraordinary" of 2 October, 1798]
Vanguard, off the Mouth of the Nile, 3 August, 1798.

My Lord,

Almighty God has blessed his Majesty's Arms in the late Battle, by a great Victory over the Fleet of the Enemy, who I attacked at sunset on the 1st August, off the Mouth of the Nile. The Enemy were moored in a strong Line of Battle for defending the entrance of the Bay, (of Shoals,) flanked by numerous Gun-boats, four Frigates, and a Battery of Guns and Mortars on an Island in their Van; but nothing could withstand the Squadron your Lordship did me the honour to place under my command. Their high state of discipline is well known to you, and with the judgement of the Captains, together with their valour, and that of the Officers and Men of every description, it was absolutely irresistible. Could anything from my pen add to the character of the Captains, I would write it with pleasure, but that is impossible.

I regret the loss of Captain Westcott of the *Majestic*, who was killed early in the Action; but the Ship was continued to be so well fought by her First Lieutenant, Mr. Cuthbert, that I have given him an order to command her till our Lordship's pleasure is known.

The Ships of the Enemy, all but their two rear Ships, are nearly dismasted: and those two, with two Frigates, I am sorry to say, made their escape: nor was it, I assure you, in my power to prevent them. Captain Hood most handsomely endeavoured to do it, but I had no Ship in a condition to support the *Zealous*, and I was obliged to call her in. The support and assistance I have received from Captain Berry cannot be sufficiently expressed. I was wounded in the head, and obliged to be carried off the deck but the service suffered no loss by that event: Captain Berry was fully equal to the important service then going on, and to him I must beg leave to refer you for every information relative to this Victory. He will present you with the Flag of the Second in Command, that of the Commander-in-Chief being burnt in *L'Orient*. Herewith I transmit you Lists of the Killed and Wounded, and the Lines of Battle of ourselves and the French. I have the honour to be, my Lord, your Lordship's most obedient Servant. HORATIO NELSON

Total - 16 Officers, 156 Seamen, 46 Marines, killed; 37 Officers, 562 Seamen, 78 Marines wounded = 895

The Officers killed and wounded on each ship were listed and in respect of the *Vanguard* were as follows:

Killed   Captain William Faddy, Marines; Mr. Thomas Seymour, Mr. John G. Taylor, Midshipmen

Wounded   Mr. Nathaniel Vassal, Mr. John M. Adye, Lieutenants; Mr. John Campbell, Admiral's Secretary; Mr. Michael Austin, Boatswain; Mr. John Weatherstone, Mr. George Antrim, Midshipmen.

Ships	Guns	Men	Killed	Injured	French Ships	Guns	Men	Outcome
Culloden	74	590			Le Guerrier	74	700	Taken
Theseus	74	590	5	30	Le Conquérant	74	700	Taken
Alexander	74	590	14	58	Le Spartiate	74	700	Taken
Vanguard	74	696	30	75	L'Aquilon	74	700	Taken
Minotaur	74	640	23	64	Le Souverein Peuple	74	700	Taken
Leander	50	343	0	14	Le Franklin	80	800	Taken
Swiftsure	74	590	7	22	L'Orient	120	1010	Burnt
Audacious	74	590	1	35	Le Tonnant	80	800	Taken
Defence	74	590	4	11	L'Heureux`	74	700	Taken
Zealous	74	590	1	7	Le Timoleon	74	700	Taken
Orion	74	590	13	29	Le Mercure	74	700	Taken
Goliath	74	590	21	41	Le Guillaume Tell	80	800	Escaped
Majestic	74	590	50	143	Le Généreux	74	700	Escaped
Bellerophon	74	590	49	148	La Diane	48	300	Escaped
La Mutine					La Justice	44	300	Escaped
Brig					L'Artemise	36	250	Burnt
					La Sérieuse	36	250	Dismasted and sunk

Master's Log (ADM 52/5316)

The cover of the log at the time of the battle includes the endorsement 'Log of HM Ship *Vanguard*. Captain Edward Berry and Tm Hardy, Esqs commencing the 12 July and ending the 26 October 1798. By Wales Clodd Master'.

The daily record shows a variety of activities in addition to the regular positions, course and weather conditions, eg. '12 July 1798 from HMS *Majestic* 10 butts of water'. Signals are listed, as are regular punishments by lash for drunkenness or fighting. 600 men engaged in vigorous activity require feeding and each opening of Pork or Beef is meticulously recorded as to identity and weight, eg.

'27 July 1798 Pork No   8935 320 lbs'
                        8943 320 lbs.'

Live beasts were also carried and on the 21st July 1798 the log records:-
'Killed 2 bullocks weighing 1100lbs No 1 556 No 2 544'

Distances sailed were recorded and, in the weeks before the battle, reflect the search, replenishing supplies at Syracuse, and the dash back to Alexandria: -

Abstracts from the log of distance covered

Date	Distance	Date	Distance	
12th July 1798	373	19th July 1798	17	Syracuse
13th July 1798	328	26th July 1798	25	
14th July 1798	299	27th July 1798	190	
15th July 1798	255	28th July 1798	22	
16th July 1798	198	29th July 1798	400	
17th July 1798	59	30th July 1798	221	
18th July 1798	88	31st July 1798	124	
		1st August 1798	30	Aboukir

VANGUARD LOG

The Navy Records Society in their publication *Great Sea Fights 1794 - 1805*, in the chapter concerning the Battle of the Nile, include the following sentence:- 'The absence of unnecessary signalling when the enemy had been sighted is very remarkable in this first fleet action in which Nelson commanded. Everyone seems to have understood exactly what he had to do, and to have been trusted to carry out his chief's intention in his own way. The fact that every captain distinguished himself was considered remarkable by Lord Howe, but was the natural result of Nelson's method."

'Wednesday, August 1st

P.M. - Moderate breezes and clear. Saw Alexandria bearing SE ½ S distant 7 or 8 leagues. Set driver. ½ past 1, set mainsail. Hauled to the wind. Unbent the best bower cable, took it out of the stern port and bent do. Again. At 4, Pharos Tower SSW distant 4 or 5 leagues. Bore up for the French fleet lying Aboukir Roads. Backed main topsail to get the *Mutine*'s boat on board. Filled do. Immediately. Soundings 15, 14, 13, 11 and 10 fathoms. 28 minutes past 6, French hoisted their colours and commenced firing on our van ships. ½ past 6, came to with the best bower in 8 fathoms and veered to ½ cable. 31 minutes past, opened our fire on the *Spartiate*, which was continued without intermission, until ½ past 8, when she struck to us. Sent Lieutenant Galwey with a party of marines to take possession of her. At 9, saw three other ships strike to the *Zealous*, *Audacious* and *Minotaur*. 55 minutes past 8 *L'Orient* took fire, the ships ahead still keeping up heavy fire on the enemy. At 10. *L'Orient* blew up with a violent explosion, and the enemy ceased their fire. 10. Let the small bower-anchor go under foot. Island being NW ½ W. Aboukir Town W ½ S. 10 minutes past 10, perceived another ship on fire, which in two minutes was extinguished, and a fresh cannonading began. 20 minutes past 10, a total cease fire for 10 minutes, when it was again renewed.

Thursday, August 2nd

A.M. – 16 minutes past 12, Lieut. Vassal went with a party of marines to take possession of another ship. 15 minutes past 2, came on board a boat from the *Alexander*. 55 minutes past 2, a total cease of firing. 28 minutes past 3, came on board a boat from the *Defence*. 40 minutes past 3, Lieut. Vassal returned, the ship he went to board having got under way before he was able to board her; picked up and brought on board 3 Frenchmen. 5 minutes past 5, the enemy's ships to the southward began firing. 54 minutes past 5, a French frigate ahead fired a broadside and struck her colours, four minutes after she was on fire, and at 7 she blew up. At 6, the *Goliath* got under way and bore down to the southward to the enemy's ships which had not struck. 40 minutes past 6, she began firing at a frigate, and continued firing until 7 o'clock. 50 minutes past 6, one of the enemy's ships of the line fired some guns and then struck her colours and was boarded. 55 minutes past, the *Zealous* weighed and went ahead. 57 minutes past 10, the English began firing at a frigate, gave her two broadsides and then ceased. ½ past 11, two French line-of-battle ships and two frigates got under way, and stood out to the sea. Total officers, seamen and marines sent to the *Spartiate*: Lieut. Galway, 3 petty officers, and 26 seamen, 1 marine officer, and 27 marines: A list of killed and wounded 3 officers, 20 seamen, and 7 marines killed, 7 officers, 60 seamen, and 8 marines wounded.

    P.M. - Moderate breezes from NW quarter, and clear weather. Employed getting down topgallant masts, yards, and topmasts, clearing the wrecks, knotting and splicing the rigging, &c. At 45 minutes past 12, the *Zealous* gave 2 ships of the line and 2 frigates which were standing out of the Bay a broadside each as she passed them. Bent the stream cable to best bower, swung ship and got the cable into its proper hawse hole. Received from .H.M.S. Culloden 3 coils of 2½ inch rope. Light winds.

Friday, August 3rd

A.M.- Moderate. Employed variously about the rigging, knotting and splicing, clearing ship, &c. Carpenters plugging up shot holes and making fishes for the main mast. Sailmakers repairing mizen staysail. 13 minutes past 10, the enemy set one of their line-of-battle ships on fire. 47 minutes past 11, she blew up. (The log continues with a summary of the ships taken and destroyed)

An account of the enemy's ships taken and destroyed on August 2nd [ie on August 1st and 2nd] 1798.

Ship's Name	Guns	Men	How disposed
Le Guerrier	74	700	Taken
Le Conquérant	74	700	Taken
Le Spartiate	74	700	Taken
L'Aquilon	74	700	Taken
Le Souverain-Peuple	74	700	Taken
Le Franklin	74	700	Taken
L'Orient	120	1010	Burnt
Le Tonnant	80	800	Taken
L'Heureux	74	700	Taken
Le Timoleon	74	700	Burnt
Le Mercure	74	700	Taken
L'Artemise	36	250	Burnt
La Sèrieuse	36	250	Dismasted sunk

CHAPTER 3

HMS *VANGUARD*

Nelson's flagship at the Battle of the Nile was in fact the fifth *Vanguard*, a 3rd rate ship-of-the-line of seventy-four guns, built at Deptford in 1787; the name *Vanguard* having been used nine times in the British Royal Navy. The name dates back to 1586 when a galleon-type ship of thirty-two guns was launched at Woolwich and given the name. She played a significant part in the campaign of the Spanish Armada in 1588, was present at the taking of Fort Crozon, near Brest, in 1594, when she flew the flag of Martin Frobisher, and off Cadiz in 1596, when she was commanded by Sir Robert Mansell.

The *Vanguard* of the Nile had seen considerable earlier service in the Channel Fleet and in the West Indies participating in the capture of Guadeloupe before refitting in Chatham in 1797. After the battle and still Nelson's flagship she was present at the capitulation of Malta in October 1798. Further service followed in the Caribbean and at Copenhagen in 1807 at the taking of the Danish Fleet. Hulked in 1812 as a receiving ship in Plymouth she was later a powder store and in 1821 was broken up after a 44-year career.

The rating of ships
The rating of ships refers to the number of guns carried. A first rate carried 100 guns upwards. A second rate carried from 84 to 100; third rate 70 to 84; fourth rate 50 to 70; fifth rate 32 to 50 and sixth rates, any number of guns up to 32 if commanded by a post-captain. (the number of the guns did vary over time).

Only ships of the first three rates were considered as ships-of-the-line, able through their armament, to be powerful enough to lie in the line of battle.

CHAPTER 4

PREPARATIONS FOR SEA

The Muster Book (ADM 36/15356)
The Muster Book containing the Table and Lists of crew and passengers is a weighty tome with cardboard cover and worn leather spine. Given the age of the document and the activity of *Vanguard* during the period of the commission it is in very good condition. Entries indicate the ship "Began Wages on 20 December 1797 and sea victualling 24 December 1797." (Just two weeks after Nelson wrote warning Berry he may be called any hour}.

The first Muster Table covers the period between 20 December 1797 and 19 February 1798 and indicate the ship was at Chatham for 6 weeks, and contains the certificate by Captain Berry, Master Clodd, Boatswain Austin and Purser Shippard:-

> 'These are to certify to the principal officers and Commissioners of his Majesty's Navy that the Articles of War and the abstracts of the Acts of Parliament were read to the Ship's Company, agreeable to the General Printed Instructions.'

A measure may be gained of the activity in preparing the ship for sea from entries such as that on the 3 February 1798 listing the requirement for one days victuals for Shipmaster Aitchinson, two boatswain, 31 riggers and 8 extra men. Between 5 and 17 February 1798 15 shipwrights and 4 boatmen with a foreman were also engaged, supplemented between the 6th and 8th of the month by 13 joiners, 2 boatmen and 3 painters. Finally on 19 February 1798 Captain Berry certified:-

> 'These are to Certify to the Commissioners for Victualling his Majesty's Navy that the supernumeries contained in the foregoing list beginning with the name Aitchinson

and ending with the name Jelico Turner being eighty three in number were actually victualled at whole allowance for all species for the times and from the dates set against their respective names in the said list. Given under my hand on the 19th February one thousand seven hundred and ninety eight. E Berry Captain

The Muster Table for the period 1 March to 30 April 1798 shows:-

Date	Where	By
1 March 1798	Blackstakes	Clerk of Cheque
8 March 1798	Nore	Clerk of Cheque
20 March 1798	Spithead	Clerk of Cheque
29 March 1798	Spithead	Clerk of Cheque
7 April 1798	At Sea	Captain and Officers
15 April 1798	At Sea	Captain and Officers
23 April 1798	At Sea	Captain and Officers
30 April 1798	At Sea	Captain and Officers

The entries indicate the officer responsible for completing the Muster and where it took place. The reference to Blackstakes refers to the deep water anchorage off Queensborough were guns would be offloaded for the shallower water passage to Chatham Dockyard and reloaded after refit had been completed. It must have been with some relief that Captain Berry and his officers took possession of the ship and shed the riggers, joiners and painters but had he been aware of the storm ahead of him he may have found space to carry some of the artisans.

Passengers
Listed as supernumerary for 2/3 allowance of provisions the following passengers are shown on the Muster as having taken advantage of the voyage south:-

'30 March 1798 Passage to Gib by order of Admiral Nelson.

    Col Montreson   24 April Lisbon
    Ensign Cadogan   24 April Lisbon
    Col Flight   30 April Ville de Paris
    Servant Felicionne   24 April Lisbon
    Servant Fleming   24 April Lisbon
    Servant Slade   24 April Lisbon'

Missing from the Book is the Muster Table and Lists for the months of May and June 1798 but as indicated elsewhere the months of July and August 1798 show the disposition and men during the period detailed in this publication.

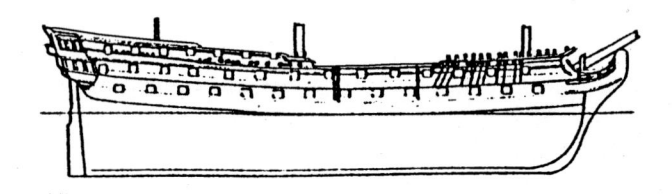

The Muster Table covering the period after the Battle shows:-

Date	Where	By
4 September 1798	At Sea	Captain and Officers
12th September 1798	At Sea	Captain and Officers
20th September 1798	At Sea	Captain and Officers
28th September 1798	Naples Bay	Captain and Officers
5th October 1798	Naples Bay	Captain and Officers
13th October 1798	Naples Bay	Captain and Officers
22nd October 1798	Marsala	Captain and Officers
30th October 1798	At Sea	Captain and Officers

Nelson wrote the following letter which was fairly accurate in respect of the *Vanguard* but proved wholly inaccurate concerning his own circumstances which proved significantly at variance with his plans!

> TO THE CAPTAINS OF SUCH OF HIS MAJESTY'S SHIPS AS MAY BE IN SEARCH OF ME; WHEN READ, TO BE ENCLOSED AND RETURNED INTO THE HANDS OF THE GOVERNOR OF SYRACUSE.
>
> *Vanguard* 7th September 1798
>
> Sir,
> I beg leave to tell you that I am on my way to Naples, where I shall be found for the next fourteen days.   I am, &c
>
> HORATIO NELSON

Muster Lists

For genealogists and historians alike, muster lists provide a useful source of information in respect of those who served as part of a ship's company. Samuel Pepys, who had a thirst for knowledge, would have appreciated the sight of students poring over Muster Books at the Public Record Office. As Secretary to the Admiralty he set in progress improvements to the professionalism of the Navy, and would have recognised and endorsed the structured process which required ships' officers to complete a weekly muster of the ship's complement. Entitlement to e.g. bounty, victualling, required proof, and the captain, purser, master and boatswain endorsed each two monthly summary enabling those who follow to verify the names of those who served their sovereign on the high seas.

The following are amongst the matters listed on the muster: - Bounty Paid - Individual Number - Date and year of entry on ship - Appearance on board - When and whether prest or not - Place and county where born (seamen only - Marines and Officers did not suffer the indignity of submitting their personal details, presumably on the basis that they were unlikely to abscond, and have to be subsequently chased) - Number and letter of tickets (in the case of men transferred to another ship) - Man's name - Qualities (see below)

Youths	under 15yrs rated **Boys** 3rd Class,
	under 18yrs, 2nd Class
	and those training as officers **Boys** 1st Class
Adults with no experience	= **Landsman**
Useful but not expert or skilful	= **Ordinary Seaman**
Able and well acquainted	= **Able Seaman**
Warrant Officer ranks	= **Boatswain Gunner Boatswain's Mate Quarter Gunner**

MUSTER TABLE (ADM 36/15356)

The Muster Table was the first page, indicating where each weekly muster had been held. The muster table used in this publication covers the eight week period 1 July to 31 August, 1798, commencing therefore at the time when Nelson and his squadron had visited Alexandria without sight or information of the French Fleet and had turned back to the North to continue the search towards Syracuse. The first four weeks of July record that the ship was 'At Sea', for the first three weeks of August that she was 'At Anchor off the Nile', and for the week ending 30th August 'At Sea'. The summary shows a complement of 595 mustered in groupings of:-

	Wk1	Wk2	Wk3	Wk4	**Wk5**	Wk6	Wk7	Wk8
Ship's Company	468	468	467	466	**445**	443	471	471
Volunteers and Boys	27	27	27	26	**23**	23	22	23
Marines' Part of Complement	93	93	93	93	**86**	86	85	85
Supernumeraries for Wages	3	3	3	3	**3**	5	15	15
Supernumeraries for Victuals	1	1	1	1	**2**	2	5	4

Week five including the Battle of the Nile records losses from the *Vanguard* muster list. Required to be signed by the Captain the muster chosen is signed by Berry's replacement, Captain Hardy, Master Clodd, Purser Shippard and Boatswain Austin, and is handsomely written in a broad copper-plate hand.

Facsimile of page from the MUSTER LIST, showing the Admiral's Retinue and

Rear Admiral Sr. Horatio Nelson K.B. Secretary and

Bounty Paid	No	Entry.	Year	Appearance.	Whence and whether Prest or not.	Place and County where Born.	Age at Time of Entry in this Ship.	No and Letter of Tickets.	MENS NAMES.	Qualities.	D.D. or R.	Time of Discharge.
		28 Mar	98	Mar 28					Sr. H. Nelson K.B.	Rear Adm.e of the Blue		
		"	"	"					John Campbell	Secretary	D.H Augt 13
		29 "		29			24		Thomas Spencer	AB		
		"		"					Thomas Allen	"		
		40 Apr		Apl 10					Arthur Leary	"		

T.M Hardy Captain
for Edward Berry Captain

Wales Clodd Master

illustrating the fine copperplate writing and formal signatures of the Ship's Officers

Year	Whither or for what Reason.	Stragling.	Necessaries supplied Marines on Shore	Venereals.	Cloaths in Sick Quarters.	Dead Mens Cloaths	Wages remitted from Abroad.	Date of the Parties Order for allotting Monthly Pay.	Two Months Advance	Slops supplied by Navy Board.	Beds.	Tobacco.	To whom the Tickets were delivered.	When Mustered. Month July / August Days 7/8 9 28 5 12 29 30
														a b c f g h i k
	98 To the Franklin French Prize & to J.H. Wilson &c?													a b c f g h
														a b c f g h i k
														a b c f g h i k
														a b c f g h i k

Alex.^r Kippard   *Purser*   *Mich.^l Austin*   *Boatswain*

LEGEND based on the Muster List H.M.S. Vanguard 1st July – 31st August 1798
ADM 36/15356

1	SURNAME	Listed in alphabetical order. Spelling, which varied considerably depending upon the writer, is according to the entry on the muster list
2	FORENAME	Abbreviated. Often it is not clear whether 'Jno' is 'John' or 'Jonathan' and whether 'Jos' is 'Joseph' or 'Joshua'
3	RANK/RATE	Abbreviated egs. PteRM = Private Royal Marines. Corp. = Corporal. Ord. = Ordinary. Qtr.Gnnr = Quarter Gunner Prest = Pressed AB = Able Seaman. LM = Landsman. C.H.Q. = Chatham Headquarters P = Portsmouth
4	NUMBER	Each man had a unique number on the list.
5	AGE	As at entry to the ship
6	WHERE BORN	As interpreted from the entry on the list
7	ENTERED	Date the man was first borne on the ships books and was paid whether or not on board
8	APPEARED	Date the man arrived on board from which he was victualled as well as paid.
9	TYPE	Whether volunteer or pressed. Or in the case of transfer the previous ship.
10	PAGE	The page on the Vanguard Muster List for the period 1st July - 31st August, 1798
	N.G.S.M.	Indicates the recipient of the Naval General Service Medal in 1848 via K. Douglas-Morris
*		Indicates inclusion of reference in the biographical notes -Section 11

1	2	3	4	5	6	7	8	9	10
ABRAHAM	George	Ord	523			06/04/98	06/04/98	Volunteer	27
ACKOUKE	Joseppe	A.B.	545	50	Malta	19/04/98	10/04/98		28
ADAMSON	William	Qtr Gunner	99	58	Plymouth	01/01/98	1/01/98	St George	5
ADDIS	Richard	LM	164	23	Wick	29/09/97	07/09/98	Enterprize	9
ADYE	Jno.M.	Lieut.	19			20/12/97	27/12/97		1
		Commissioned 20/12/97 **Listed as wounded in the official dispatch**							
ALBORE	Jno.	A.B.	461	22	Finland	05/03/98	05/03/98	St. George	24
ALLEN*	Thomas	A.B.				29/03/98	29/03/98		39
	Admiral's Retinue								
ANTRAM	George	Mdshpmn	504			10/03/98	17/03/98	Enterprize	26
	N.G.S.M.	Listed as wounded in the official dispatch							
ARNOLD	Richard	Qtr Gnnr	108	53	Malton	01/01/98	01/01/98	St George	6
ATKINS	James	LM	294	20	Epsom, Surrey	11/12/98	02/03/98	Volunteer	15
ATKINSON	Charles	QtrMstrs	62	42	Gateshead	25/11/97	01/01/98	Monmouth	4
		Mate to 01/07/98 then Qtr Mstr						Victory	
AUSTIN*	Michael	Boatswain	243			25/01/98	25/01/98		13
					Listed as wounded in the official dispatch		Discharged 02/10/98		
AVREENS	Anthony	LM	207	20	Madeira	08/10/97	07/01/98	Rosario	11
BAILEY	Charles	LM	379	35	London	16/02/98	04/03/98	Volunteer	19
BAKEWELL	Robt.	Pte.R.M.	86			04/01/98	04/01/98	C.H.Q.	37
BANTON	Leon	A.B.	440	32	Norwich	05/03/98	05/03/98	St. George	22
	N.G.S.M.								
BAPTISO	Jn	LM	185	20	Genoa	08/10/97	07/01/98	Rosario	10
BARBER	Thos.	Ord	490	22	Shrewsbury	05/03/98	05/03/98	St.George	25

61

1	2	3	4	5	6	7	8	9	10
BAREUP	Andw.S.	LM	464	41	Mantua	05/03/98	05/03/98	St.George	24
BARKER	Arthr.	LM	308	27	Northwich	28/12/87	02/03/98	Volunteer	16
	Killed in action 01/08/98								
BARNES	Thos.	A.B.	74	33	Norwich	25/11/97	01/01/98	Monmouth/Victory	4
	To 01/05/98 then Gunners Mate								
BARNETT	Richd.	A.B.	38	40	Helstone	01/01/98	01/01/98	St George	2
BARNETT (2nd)	Richd	LM	154	32	London	28/09/97	07/01/98	Volunteer Enterprize	8
BARRETT	Thos.	A.B.	38	21	Portsmouth	25/11/97	01/01/98		2
BARRY	Thos.	A.B.	475	38	Co.Wexford	05/03/98	05/03/98	St George	24
BARTLETT	Rich.	LM	302	29	London	26/12/97	02/3/98	Volunteer	16
BATLIN	Thos.	PteRM	97			19/03/98	20/03/98	P.H.Q.	37
	Killed in Action 01/08/98								
BEALE	Fras.	A.B.	111	24	Berkshire	01/01/98	01/01/98	St.George	6
	Killed in Action 01/08/98								
BENNETT	Jno	A.B	244	22	London	02/01/98	21/01/98	Volunteer London	13
	Ord. To 30/03/98 Then A.B								
	Discharged 04/08/98 Lent with Captain being his servant 05/08/98								
BENTLY	Jno	LM	363	21	Derbyshire	03/03/98	04/03/98	Volunteer	19
BERRY *	Edwd.	Capt.	20			20/12/97	29/12/97		1
	Commission 20/12/97 Sent with dispatches to England by Adl. H. Nelson Aug 5th 1798								
BESCOBY	Thos.	Sgt R.M.	3			31/12/97	31/12/97	C.H.Q	34
	Sgt to 26/05/98 then Private to 2/8/98 then Sgt								
BIRCH	Jas.	Ord	537	20	Exmouth	19/04/98	19/04/98	Volunteer	27
BIRCH	Jesse	Pte R.M.	67			04/01/98	04/01/98	C.H.Q.	36
	Died of wounds received in Action 05/08/98								

62

1	2	3	4	5	6	7	8	9	10
BIRMINGHAM	Jas	Pte.R.M.	14			31/12/97	31/12/97		34
BLAKEY	Wm.		437	49	Essex	05/03/98	05/03/98	St.George	22
	Carpenters Crew								
BLAND	Wm.	Pte.R.M.	35			31/12/97	31/12/97	C.H.Q.	35
BOCOCK	Thos.	LM	170	28	Chatham	27/09/97	07/01/98		9
BOSWELL	Jas.	A.B.	58	25	Kilcawdy	25/11/97	01/01/98		4
BOTTLE	Soloman	A.B.	412	34	Somerset	05/03/98	05/03/98	St.George	21
BOTWRIGHT	Jas.	A.B.	52	31	Acle, Norfolk	05/03/98	05/03/98	St.George	23
BOWES	Law	A.B.	388	48	Dublin	05/03/98	05/03/98	St.George	20
BOYD	Jno.	A.B.	413	25	Bristol	05/03/98	05/03/98	St.George	21
	Discharged 05/10/98 B.N.430								
BOYD	Robt.	A.B.	420	30	Bristol	05/03/98	05/03/98	St.George	21
BOYNETT	Peter	LM	163	21	London	26/09/97	07/01/98	Volunteer Enterprize	9
BRAGG	John	Qtr Gnnr	144	35	W/haven	01/01/98	01/01/98	St.George	8
	Discharged 13/08/98 to *Orion* to be conveyed to Hospital see Orion muster page 42								
BRAND	Josh.	A.B.	476	29	London	05/03/98	05/03/98	St.George	24
BRIGHT	Jas.	A.B	431	30	London	05/03/98	05/03/98	St.George	22
	To 01/05/98 then Yeoman of Sheets								
BRIGHT	Richd.	LM	333	20	Shrewsbry Roddington	03/01/98	02/03/98	Volunteer	17
BROERS	Johanna	Pte R.M.	61			04/01/98	04/01/98	C.H.Q.	36
BROOKS	Natl.	LM	349	22	Weymouth	02/02/98	04/03/98	Vol	18
BROWN	Anty.	A.B.	103	32	Halifax	01/01/98	01/01/98	St.George	6

1	2	3	4	5	6	7	8	9	10
BROWN	Jas.	LM	538	20	London	19/04/98	10/04/98	Volunteer Diadem pg.41	27
BROWN	Jno.	LM	300	21	Birmnghm	04/12/97	02/03/98	Volunteer	15
BROWN	Saml.	A.B. A.B. to 28/04/98 then Mid.	35	35	Cstle Donn	25/11/97	01/01/98		2
BROWN	Thos.	LM	366	22	London	05/02/98	04/03/98	Volunteer	19
BROWNE	Robt.	A.B.	83	22	Hull	25/11/97	01/01/98	Monmouth/Victory	5
BROWNING	Jno	PteRM	57			04/01/98	04/01/98		35
BRUISSINE	Garrett	Pte.R.M.	93			04/01/98	04/01/98	C.H.Q.	37
BRYANT	Geo.	A.B.	86	30	Plymouth	01/01/98	01/01/98	St.George	5
BRYANT	Jno.	Boy3rd	5	12	Plymouth	01/01/98	01/01/98	St.George	17
BUCKLE	Wm.	LM LMto 01/05/98 then carpenter's crew	338	21	London 12/02/98		02/05/98	Volunteer	17 21
BUCKLEY	Benjn. N.G.S.M.	Pte.R.M	91			04/01/98	04/01/98	C.H.Q.	37
BUDD	Jno.	Boy 2nd Discharged 13/08/98 to Ships Books No. 562	12	19	Portsmth	30/03/98	30/03/98		32
BULL	Jno.	LM	520	22	Amsterdam	06/04/98	06/04/98	Montague Ref. Page 40	22
BURCH	Salvo	A.B.	552	42	Malta	19/04/98	19/04/98		28
BURKE	Lawc.	A.B.	82	23	Quebec	25/11/97	01/01/98	Monmouth/Victory	5
BURNE	Jno.	LM	297	28	Co.Wicklow	25/12/97	02/03/98	Volunteer	15
BURROWS	Wm N.G.S.M.	Pte. R.M.	42			31/12/97	31/12/97	C.H.Q	35
BUTLER	Geo.	Ordy.	265	21	Isle of Man	12/01/98	02/03/98	Volunteer	14

1	2	3	4	5	6	7	8	9	10
BUTLER	Mattw.	Ordy.	493	24	Dublin	05/03/98	05/03/98	St.George	25
BUTLER	Wm.	Pte.R.M.	9			31/12/97	31/12/97	C.H.Q.	34
BUTLER	Wm.	LM	364	20	Tavington Berkshire	03/02/98	04/03/98	Volunteer	19
BYSON	John	Ord.	532	28	Glasgow	19/04/98	19/04/98	Volunteer	27
CAMPBELL	John	Sec.				28/03/98	28/03/98	39	

Secretary Admiral's retinue Discharged 12/08/98 to the *Franklin* – French prize of Sir H.Nelson KB

Listed as wounded in the official dispatch

CAPEL	*Hon.T.Bladen Lieut.		524			05/04/98	11/04/98		27

N.G.S.M. Acting Ord. From RA Nelson 05/04/98 Discharged 13/08/98 on Promotion.

CAPELLO	Jno.	A.B.	541	45	Malta	19/04/98	19/04/98		28
CARDEN	Jno.	LM	368	23	Lingfield	04/03/98	04/03/98	Volunteer	19

To 01/05/98 then carpenter's crew

CARNEY	Jno.	Ord.	534	26	London Also page 40	19/04/98	19/04/98	Volunteer	27
CARNELL	Jno.	LM	285	20	Ramsey Huntingdon	29/09/97	29/09/97	Volunteer 1	5
CAVE	Berry	LM	173	22	Welden	03/10/97	03/10/97	Volunteer Enterprize	9

Carpenters crew wef 01/05/98

CEASER	Jno.	Ord.	225	28	Bombay	07/11/97	07/01/98	'Ruby'	12
CHALTON	Jno.	LM	201	27	Manchestr	11/04/97	07/01/98	Volunteer Lincoln	11
CHAMPION	Chas.	Mid.	259			17/02/98	19/02/98		13

Mid. To 30/03/98 then Ord. To 01/05/98 the Mid. *Vanguard* Officers pay list

CHRISTIAN	Wm.	A.B.	130	26	Isle of Man	01/01/98	01/01/98	St.George	7
CLARE	Michl.	Ord.	267	20	Dublin	09/02/97	02/03/98	Volunteer	14

65

1	2	3	4	5	6	7	8	9	10
CLARK	Forbes	LM	313	27	Armagh	29/12/97	02/03/98	Volunteer	16
CLAYTON	Jas.	A.B.	104	59	Shoreham	01/01/98	01/01/98	St.George	1
CLODD*	Wales	Master Warrant 21/12/97	2			24/12/97	24/12/97		1
COATES	John	LM	161	20	London	26/09/97	07/01/98	Volunteer Enterprize	9
COBBLESTONE	Jno.	Boy3rd	10	13	Fowy	16/11/97	07/01/98	Scipio/Zealand	33
COGAR	Edwd.	Caulker Officers Warrant 28/02/98	499	43	Plymouth	05/03/98	05/03/98		25
COLEMAN	Chris.	A.B.	454	25	Suffolk	05/03/98	05/03/98	St.George	23
COLLIER	Fras.A N.G.S.M.	Boy1st	7			21/03/98	21/03/98	Volunteer	31
COMPTON*	Heny.	Lieut. Commission 27/01/98	249			27/01/98	03/02/98		13
COMYN*	Rev. Stephen G.Chaplain Officers Warrant 02/03/98		514			22/03/98	31/03/98		26
CONNELL	Jas. **Killed in Action 01/08/98**	LM	194	32	Cork	13/04/97	07/01/98	Lincoln substitute	10
CONNELL	Wm.	LM	377	32	Cork	15/02/98	04/03/98	Volunteer	19
CONNELLY	Danl.	A.B.	389	22	Dublin	05/03/98	05/03/98	St. George	20
CONNELLY(2nd)	Jas.	Ord.	271	24	Cork	17/02/98	02/03/98	Prest.	14
CONNER	Patk.	PteRM	33			31/12/97	31/12/97	C.H.Q	35
CONNER	Wm.	A.B.	392	20	Dublin	05/03/98	05/03/98	St.George	20
COOK	Thos.	A.B.	463	36	Yarmouth	05/03/98	05/03/98	St.George	24
COONAHAN	Danl. **Killed in Action 01/08/98**	LM	150	49	Donerail	23/09/97	07/01/98	Sandwich	8

1	2	3	4	5	6	7	8	9	10
COOPER	Heny.	Boy 1st	9			28/03/98	28/03/98	Volunteer	31
COOPER	Jno.	Carpenter	263			03/03/98	03/03/98		14
		Warrant 03/03/98							
CORALAN	Chris.	PteRM	65			04/01/98	04/01/98	C.H.Q.	36
CORK	Jno.	LM	316	23	Bradfield	30/12/97	02/03/98	Volunteer	16
		LM to 01/05/98 then Carpenters Crew							
COTTON	Saml.	Surgs.Mate	22			25/12/97	25/12/97		2
		Officers Warrant 21/12/97							
COUKE	Fras.	A.B.	557	23	Malta	20/5/98	23/05/98		28
	Killed in Action 01/08/98								
COX	Thos.	LM	298		Yorkshire	25/12/97	02/03/98	Volunteer	15
COXHEAD	Jas.	LM	357	20	London	02/02/98	04/03/98		18
	N.G.S.M.	Greenwich Pensioner No 161 (under name Joseph Burgin)							
CRABB	Jno.	LM	187	23	Exeter	08/10/97	15/01/98	Prest Prince Frederick	10
CRADEN	Richd.	LM	155	21	Bucks.	28/09/97	07/01/98	Volunteer Enterprize	8
	N.G.S.M.								
CREASY	Jas.	LM	289	20	Wisbech	17/12/97	02/03/98	Volunteer	15
CULLEN	Jno	PteRM	100			19/03/98	20/03/98	P.H.Q.	37
CUPARA	Guispr.	A.B.	544	37	Malta	19/04/98	19/04/98		28
DAND	Willm.	LM	221	50	Rochester	07/11/97	07/01/98	Ruby	5
DANIELS	Thos.	PteRM	44			31/12/97	31/12/97	C.H.Q.	35
DAVIDSON	Thos.	LM	182	20	London	08/10/97	07/01/98	Rosario	10
DAVIES	David	A.B.	92	40	Flintshire	01/01/98	01/01/98	St.George	5
	N.G.S.M.	to 01/05/98 then Qtr Gnnr.							

1	2	3	4	5	6	7	8	9	10
DAVIES (1ST)	Wm.	LM	380	20	Essex	16/02/98	04/03/98	Substitute	19
DAWSON	Fra.	A.B.	71	33	Berwick	25/11/97	01/01/98	Monmouth Victory	4
DAWSON	Willm.	Gnnr.	5			24/12/97	24/12/97		1
DEACON	Geo.	A.B.	416	28	Bristol	05/03/98	05/03/98	St.George	21
DEALE	Wm.	LM	361	20	Antrim	16/01/98	04/03/98	Volunteer	19
DEFFIE	Ian	Ord.	494	40	Isle of France	05/03/98	05/03/98	St.George	25
DELLAMORE	Jas.	LM	384	22	Walpole	20/02/98	04/03/98	Volunteer	20
DELTON	Johan A	PteRM	82			04/01/98	04/91/98	C.H.Q.	37
DEMARE	Samfield	LM	184	20	Malta	08/10/97	07/01/98	Rosario	10
DENSE	Thos.	Boy3rd	9	19	Sheffield	16/11/97	07/01/98	Scipio/Zealand	33
DEPEAR	Jno.	LM	309	23	London	28/12/97	02/03/98	Volunteer	16
DEWY	Richd.	PteRM	99			19/03/98	20/03/98		37
DICKIE	Fras.	PteRM	31			31/12/97	31/12/97		35
Killed in Action 01/08/98									
DISTANT	Jno.	LM	25	20	Kensington	29/12/97	29/12/97		2
DIGLASH	Robt.	A.B.	67	24?34?	Edinburgh	25/11/97	01/01/98	Monmouth/Victory	4
DILMINA	Dora	A.B.	553	23	Malta	19/04/98	19/04/98		28
DORMAND	Jno.	Qtr Gnnr	65	50	Lancashire	25/11/97	01/01/98	Monmouth/Victory	4
DORRINGTON	Wm.	A.B.	223	25	Stafford	07/11/97	07/01/98	Ruby	12
DOUGLAS	Geoe.	LM	186	20	Brentford	08/10/97	07/01/98	Prest	10
DOWLING	Jas.	Boy3rd	4	13	Plymouth	01/01/98	01/01/98	St.George	33
DOWLING	Jas.	A.B.	90	30	Falmouth	01/01/98	01/01/98	St.George	5
DOWNS	Thos.	LM	346	28	London	28/01/98	04/03/98		18
DOYLE	Jno	A.B.	52	32	London	25/11/97	01/01/98	Monmouth/Victory	3

1	2	3	4	5	6	7	8	9	10
DREW	Heny.	A.B.	385	45	Cornwall St. Mawes	05/03/98	05/03/98	St/George	20
DUCKER	Jno.	LM	314	34	Belton Lincolnshire	29/12/97	02/03/98	Volunteer	16
DUDLEY	Richd.	A.B.	114	45	Cork	01/01/98	01/01/98	St.George	6
DUNN	Jno.	LM	362	20	Kings County	25/10/97	04/03/98	Prest	19
DYKE	Jno.	LM	282	20	Hatton Warwickshire	22/09/97	02/03/98	Volunteer	15
EAMES	Michl.	Ord.	489	39	Ireland Ballyshannon	05/03/98	05/03/98	St.George	25
ELD	Jno.	PteRM	54			04/01/97	04/01/97	C.H.Q.	35
ELLESBY	Wm.	LM	319	29	Odiham	30/12/97	02/03/98	Volunteer	16
ELLICK	Fras.	A.B.	465	33	Jersey	05/03/98	05/03/98	St.George	24
ELLIOT	Danl.	PteRM	11			31/12/97	31/12/97	C.H.Q	34
ELLIOT	Peter	PteRM	17			31/12/97	31/12/97	C.H.Q.	3
ELMORE	Wm.	Boy2nd	2	16	Chatham	03/01/98	03/01/98	Argonaut	32
						Discharged 13/08/98 Defence			
ENGLISH	Wm.	Caulkers Mate	246	29	Chatham	26/01/98	27/01/98	Sandwich pay list 1	3
ENGLISH	Jas.	QtrGnnr	121	42	Yorkshire	01/01/98	01/01/98	St.George	7
		To 01/05/98 then Yeoman in powder room.							
ENNESS	Jno.	PteRM	87			04/01/98	04/01/98	C.H.Q.	37
ESTRA	Juan	LM				11/06/98	11/06/98		42
		H.Courier of Cadiz prize from *Alexander*							

1	2	3	4	5	6	7	8	9	10
EVANS	Wm. N.G.S.M.	A.B.	397	23	Exeter	05/03/98	05/03/98	St.George	20
EYRES	Jno.	PteRM	85			04/01/98	04/01/98	C.H.Q.	37
		To 01/07/98 the Corporal							
FADEN	Hugh	CorpRM	5			31/12/97	31/12/97	C.H.Q.	34
		To 26/05/98 then Sgt to 02/08/98 then Private							
FADDY*	Wm.	CaptRM	47			04/01/98	04/01/98	C.H.Q.	35
	Killed in Action 01/08/98								
FADDY	Wm.	Mid.				02/04/98	02/04/98		26
	Discharged 14/04/98 to Boy1st					23/05/98	23/05/98		28
FARRELL	Jno.	LM	212	42	Dublin	15/10/97	07/01/98	Prince Frederick	11
FIELD	Heny.	A.B.	124	28	Drogheda	01/01/98	01/01/98	St.George	7
		To 01/05/98 the Qtr Gunner							
FINLAY	Peter	A.B.	129	30	London	01/01/98	01/01/98	St.George	7
FITZPATRICK	Chas.	PteRM	27			31/12/97	31/12/97	C.H.Q.	35
FITZPATRICK	Jno.	A.B.	387	25	Dublin	05/03/98	05/03/98	St.George	20
		To 01/05/98 then Qtr Gunner							
FLEMING	John	A.B.	96	37	Torpoint	01/01/98	01/01/98	St.George	5
FLINT	Pedro	A.B.	467	24	Sweden	05/03/98	05/03/98	St.George	24
FOLEY	Patk.	Ord.	518	29	Dublin	06/04/98	06/04/98	Tender	26
								Favourite Nancy	40
FORSTER	Jas.	LM	530	20	Carlisle	19/04/98	19/04/98	Volunteer	27
	Killed in Action 01/08/98							See also	40
FOX	Robt.	LM	359	21	Bethnal Green	02/02/98	19/04/98	Volunteer See also 40	27

1	2	3	4	5	6	7	8	9	10
FRANCE	Jno.	LM	213	22	Blackburn	15/10/97	07/01/98	Prince Frederick	11
FRANKFULL	Wm.	LM	203	20	Tiverton	10/04/97	07/01/98	Lincoln substitute	11
FULLER	Thos.	LM	165	24	Andover	29/09/98	07/01/98	Volunteer Enterprize	9
FURBER	Thos.	Mid	23			29/12/97	29/12/97	America	2
						Discharged 25/03/98			
GALWAY*	Edw.	Lt.	18			20/12/97	27/12/97		1
		Commission 20th December 1797							
GARDINER	Jno.	Msrs Mate	227			07/11/97	07/01/88	Ruby	12
		To 11/01/98 then Midshipman to 25/02/98 then Masters Mate							
GARDNER	Jno.	A.B.	102	55	Plymouth	01/01/98	01/01/98	St.George	6
GARLAND	Isaac	Ord.	485	22	Gloucester	05/03/98	05/03/98	St.George	25
GARLAND	Richd.	Ord	268	37	Longford Ireland	11/02/98	11/02/98	Late Enterprize	14
GATHERS	Chas.	A.B.	40	44	London	25/11/97	01/01/98		2
		To 05/05/98 then Quarter gunners mate							
GEARY	Jno.	A.B.	473	44	Co Cork	05/03/98	05/03/98	St. George	24
GEE	Joseph	PteRM	80			04/01/98	04/01/98	C.H.Q.	36
GEORGE	Richd.	LM	354	20	Wiltshire	31/01/98	04/03/98	Volunteer	18
GIBBONS	Patk.	PteRM	40			31/12/97	31/12/97	C.H.Q	35
GIBBS	Saml.	A.B.	456	26	Yarmouth	05/03/98	05/03/98	St.George	23
GIBBS	Thos.	Ord.	483	21	London	05/03/98	05/03/98	St.George	25
GILES	Richd.	A.B.	138	25	Bristol	01/01/98	01/01/98	St.George	7
GILES	Thos.	LM	295	28	Goring Ireland	12/12/97	02/03/98	Volunteer	15
GLYNN	Andw.	QtrMsts	404	28	Glasgow	05/03/98	05/03/98	St.George	21
		Mate to 01/05/98 then QuarterMaster							

71

1	2	3	4	5	6	7	8	9	10
GODDRAM	Thos.	LM	528	20	Kent	19/04/98	19/04/98	Volunteer	27
								See also	40
GOLDFINCH	Jas.	A.B.	447	25	Yarmouth	05/03/98	05/03/98	St.George	23
GOLIA	Fras.	A.B.	547	48	Malta	19/04/98	19/04/98		28
GORDAN 1st	Wm.	Ord.	269	36	Peterhead	09/02/98	02/03/98	Substitute	14
		To 01/05/98 then Carpenter's Crew Scotland							
GORE	Rich.	Carpentrs	14	28	Stroud	24/12/97	24/12/97	Volunteer	1
		Crew Discharged 17/08/98 to H.M.S. Emerald on promotion							
GORMAN	Thos.	A.B.	478	54	Bristol	05/03/98	05/03/98	St.George	24
GOVVIETT	Robert	A.B.	100	26	Newcastle	01/01/98	01/01/98	St.George	5
		To 01/05/98 then QuarterMaster's Mate							
GRAHAM	Danl.	PteRM	79			04/01/98	04/01/98	C.H.Q.	36
GRATTON	Geo.	PteRM	12			31/12/97	31/12/97	C.H.Q.	34
GRAVISE	Fras.	A.B.	549	22	Malta	19/04/98	19/04/98		28
GREEK	Joseppe	A.B.	542	24	Malta	19/04/98	19/04/98		28
GREEN	Thos.	PteRM	16			31/12/97	31/12/97	C.H.Q.	34
GRIFFIN	Jos.	LM	296	24	Deptford	23/12/97	02/03/98	Volunteer	15
GRIFFITHS	Jno.	PteRM	41			31/12/97	31/12/97	C.H.Q.	35
GRIMSHAW	Jno.	LM	283	23	Liverpool	22/09/97	02/03/98	Volunteer	15
GROSE	Walter	A.B.	396	25	Minnegizzy	05/03/98	05/03/98	St.George	20
GUBBINS	Thos.	PteRM	28			31/12/97	31/12/97	C.H.Q.	35
GUNNER	Garrett	Ord.	240	20	Cork	16/01/98	20/01/98	Royal William	12
GUNTERY	Jno.	LM	191	28	London	13/04/97	07/01/98	Lincoln Substitute	10
HAGERTY	Danl.	A.B.	432	35	Cork	05/03/98	05/03/98	St.George	22

1	2	3	4	5	6	7	8	9	10
HAGGETT	John	LM	350	38	Goludy Perthshire	31/01/98	04/03/98	Volunteer	18
HAINSCOTT	Jno.	Ord.	522	20	London	06/04/98	06/04/98	Prest. Diadem See page 40	27
HAIR	Ivey	LieutRM	49			04/01/97	04/01/97	C.H.Q.	35
HALL	Fras.	A.B.	394	23	Cornwall	05/03/98	05/03/98	St.George	20
HALL	Jas.	Boy2nd	10	16	London	05/02/98	05/02/98	Volunteer	32
HALL	Robert N.G.S.M.	LM	177	20	London	03/10/97	07/01/98	VolunteerEnterprize	9
HALLOWS	Heny.	PteRM	75			04/01/98	04/01/98	C.H.Q.	12
HAMMOND	Anty.	Ord.	229	22	Barbados	16/11/97	07/01/98	Scipio-Zealand	12
HAMMOND	Geo.	Ord.	488	20	Plymouth	05/03/98	05/03/98	St.George	25
		Lent to La. Fortune French prize 12/08/98							
HAMMOND	Jno.	A.B.	64	31	Shepton Mallett	25/11/97	01/01/98	Monmouth/Victory	4
HAND	Jno.	Ord.	497	39	County of West Mead	05/03/98	05/03/98	St.George	25
HANLON	James	Boy 2nd	1	13	Hampshire	01/01/98	01/01/98	Monmouth Victory	32
HANSELL	Wm.	PteRM	30			31/12/97	31/12/97	C.H.Q.	35
HARDY	Josh.	Ord.	536	20	London	19/04/98	19/04/98	Volunteer See also page 40	27
HARDY	Thos.M	Captain				02/08/98	06/08/98		42
		(after Berry *La Mutine* brig acting orders Sir H. Nelson K.B.)							
HARNAUGHSY	Patk.	LM	175	31	Ballymore	03/10/97	07/01/98	VolunteerEnterprize	9
HARRIS	Jno.	PteRM	84			04/01/98	04/01/98	C.H.Q.	37

1	2	3	4	5	6	7	8	9	10
HART	Richd. N.G.S.M.	PteRM	19			31/12/97	31/12/97	C.H.Q.	34
HARTLAND	Jno.	A.B.	477	40	Bristol	05/03/98	05/03/98	St.George	24
HASDEN	Jno.	A.B.	430	30	London	05/03/98	05/03/98	St.George	22
HASSA	Johan	A.B.	546	45	Malta	19/04/98	19/04/98		28
HATHWOOD	Robt.	LM	355	20	Fulham	01/02/98	04/03/98	Volunteer	18
HAWES	Thos.	A.B.	439	34	Sudbury	05/03/98	05/03/98	St.George	22
HENDERSON	Edwd.	A.B.	75	26	Isle of Man	25/11/97	01/01/98	Monmouth/Victory	4
HENLEY	Thos.	PteRM	92			04/01/98	04/01/98	C.H.Q.	37
HEXTRAM	Jno.	A.B.	469	38	Sweden	05/03/98	05/03/98	St.George	24
HICKSON	Jno.	PteRM	55			04/01/98	04/01/98	C.H.Q.	35
HILL	Josh.	Boy 2nd	9	16	Huntoro Kent	05/02/98	05/02/98	Volunteer	32
HIMAS	Thos.	Boy 3rd 14	17		Foulsham Kent	14/01/98	14/01/98	Volunteer	33
HILL	Jonathan	Ord.	237	29	London	09/01/98	09/01/98	Volunteer	12
HOBBS	John	LM	351	18	Isle of Wight	31/01/98	04/03/98	Volunteer	18
HOCK	Jno.	Qtr Gnnr To 01/05/98 then Yeoman Powder Room	87	42	Plymouth	01/01/98	01/01/98	St.George	5
HOLBERT	Jno.	PteRM	78			04/01/98	04/01/98	C.H.Q.	36
HOLDER	Richd.	LM	352	20	Pensfort Somerset	31/01/98	04/03/98	Volunteer	18
HOLLAND	Jno.	LM	193	38	London	13/04/98	07/01/98	Lincoln substitute	10

1	2	3	4	5	6	7	8	9	10
HONEY	Wm.	LM	347	24	London	29/01/98	04/03/98	Volunteer	18
HOOPER	Jno.	Ord.	491	37	Plymouth	05/03/98	05/03/98	St.George	25
HOPE	Saml.	PteRM	83			04/01/98	04/01/98	C.H.Q.	37
HORSLER	Josh.	PteRM	56			04/01/98	04/01/98	C.H.Q.	35
HOWMAN	Petr.	LM	293	26	Ryeboro' Norfolk	01/12/97	02/03/98	Volunteer	15
HUDSON	Thos.	LM	327	20	Dublin	23/12/97	02/03/98	Volunteer	17
HUGES	Thos.	PteRM	59			04/01/98	04/01/98	C.H.Q.	35
HUGGETT	Wm.	PteRM	68			04/01/98	04/01/98	C.H.Q.	36
HUGHES	Willm.	LM	245	33	Kilkenny	26/01/98	26/01/98	Volunteer London	13
HUGHES 2nd	Wm.	A.B.	512	30	Kilkenny	25/03/98	25/03/98	Formidable	26
HUNT	Thos. N.G.S.M.	LM	197	20	London	15/04/97	07/01/98	substitute Lincoln	10
HUNT	Jas.	LM	158	26	Birm'ham	23/09/97	23/09/97	Volunteer	8
HURST	Thos.	PteRM	81			04/01/98	04/01/98	C.H.Q.	37
HUTCHINSON	Wm.	LM	277	20	Dundee	20/12/97	02/03/98	Volunteer	14
HYDER	Condl.	A.B.	472	27	Hanover	05/03/98	05/03/98	St.George	24
INFIELD	Cabel	A.B.				18/02/98	18/02/98	Volunteer	13
		AB to 30/03/98 then Midshipman Discharged 13/08/98 on promotion							
ISAACSON	Stut. N.G.S.M.	Clerk	21	24	London	29/12/97	29/12/97	Prest Zealand pay list	2
IVES	Clement	Mid	511			23/03/98	23/03/98		26
JACKSON	Wm N.G.S.M.	Ord	256	20	London	15/2/98	15/2/98	Volunteer	13
JAMES	Michl	AB	474	40	Cornwall	05/03/98	05/03/98	St George	24

75

1	2	3	4	5	6	7	8	9	10
JEFFERSON	Mich.	Surgeon Warrant 23/12/97	15			23/12/97	24/12/97		1
JEFFRIES	Benjm.	AB	101	45	Plymouth Dock	01/01/98	01/01/98	St. George	6
JENKINS	Richd.	Drummer R.M.				31/12/97	31/12/97	C.H.Q	34
JOHNSON	Jas.	Qtr Gnnr	63	27	Hull	25/11/97	01/01/98	Monmouth/Victory	4
JOHNSON	Thos.	Boatswain Mate	501	31	Portsmth	06/03/98	10/03/98	Zealand/St. George	26
JOHNSON	Wm.	AB	508	23	Newcastle	22/03/98	22/03/98	Volunteer	26
JOINER	Thos.	AB to 01/05/98 then Boatswains Mate	507	23	Hull	22/03/98	22/03/98	Volunteer	26
JONES	Edwd.	LM	323	34	Derbyshire	31/12/97	02/03/98	Volunteer	17
JONES	Philip	Ord	481	22	Bristol	05/03/98	05/03/98	St. George	25
JONES	Philip	Ord	344	22	Guadaloupe	09/12/97	02/03/98	Boreas	18
JONES	Robt.	Boy 2nd	8	15	Birmingham	19/01/98	19/01/98	Volunteer	32
JONES	Thos.	LM.	306	26	Northmptn	28/12/97	02/03/98	Prest	16
JONES	Wm.	Ord	525	25	Monmouth	19/04/98	19/04/98		27
KEELAN	Wm.	LM	429	22	Barram Kent	19/04/98 Lent to *La Fortune* French Prize 12/08/98	19/04/98	Volunteer	27
KEENAN	Barney **Killed in Action 01/08/98**	AB	391	36	Dublin	05/03/98	05/03/98	St. George	20
KELLY	Richd.	LM	358	30	London	02/02/98	04/03/98		18
KELLY	Wm.	PteRM				19/03/98	20/03/98	P.H.Q.	38

1	2	3	4	5	6	7	8	9	10
KEMP	Edwd.	LM	360	28	Mulbarton Norfolk	13/01/98	04/03/98	Volunteer	18
KENCH	Jno.	LM	336	20	Northmptn	24/01/98	02/03/98	Volunteer	17
KENDLE	Thos.	AB to 01/05/98 then Sailmakers crew	79	26	Guernsey	25/11/97	01/01/98		4
KENNEDY	Danl.	Qtr Gnnr To 01/05/98 then S. Corporal	88	45	London Derry	01/01/98	01/01/98	St. George	5
KENNEDY	Edwd.	LM	326	24	County Tipperary	16/12/97	02/03/98	Volunteer	17
KENNY	Jas.	Ord	496	28	Dublin	05/03/98	05/03/98	St. George	25
KERBY	Wm.	Boy 2nd 4	16		Coventry	16/11/97	07/01/98	Scipio Zealand	32
KIRKLAND	Wm.	LM	310	21	Tame Oxfordshire	28/12/97	02/03/98	Volunteer	16
KNIGHT	John	LM	343	23	London	08/10/97	02/03/98	Volunteer	18
KYLE	Jno.	LM	381	31	Manchstr	16/02/98	04/03/98	Substitute	20
LADNOR	Jno.	LM	539	20	Deal	19/04/98	19/04/98	Volunteer Diadem	27
LAMB	Jno.	LM.	292	35	Spalding	24/11/97	02/03/98	Prest.	15
LAMBERT	Nichs.	AB	120	25	Dublin	01/01/98	01/01/98	St. George	6
Died 09/08/98 of Wounds received in Action									
LANCASTER	Robert	AB	94	49	Liverpool	01/01/98	01/01/98	St. George	5
Killed in Action 01/08/98									
LANCASTER	Thos.	AB	427	27	Bristol	05/03/98	05/03/98	St. George	22
LANGTON Thos	LM	280	20		London	25/12/97	02/03/98		14
LAWLER	Patk.	LM	218	29	Co Kerry	19/10/97	07/01/98	**Sandwich**	11
LAWLER	Powel	Pte RM	88			04/01/98	**04/01/98**	C.H.Q.	37

77

1	2	3	4	5	6	7	8	9	10
LEARY	Arthr.	LM	374	28	Co Cork	14/02/98	04/03/98		19
	\multicolumn{9}{l}{Admiral's list Discharged 13/04/98 Re-enter 14/04/98 from Books No.37A}								
LEARY	Jerm.	AB	411	27	London	05/03/98	05/03/98	St.George	21
	Killed in action 01/08/98								
LEE	Robt.Orman	Boy 2nd	11	14	London	04/03/98	04/03/98		32
								Lent to French prize Franklin Aug 98	
LEGG	Danl.	2nd MstrsM	61	37	Aberdeen	25/11/97	01/01/98	Monmouth/Victory	4
	Killed in Action 01/08/98								
LEVOIN	Jno.	LM	172	23	London	03/10/97	07/01/98	VolunteerEnterprize	9
LEWES	Danl.	AB	39	26	London	25/11/97	01/01/98		2
LILLY	Mishach	LM	157	20	Southwold	03/09/97	07/01/98	Prest	8
LINDSAY	Peter	Ord	535	20	Glain	19/04/98	19/04/98	Prest	27
	Also listed @ 18 in Supernumerary list Scotland								
LLOYD	Jno.	LM	320	23	Deptford	30/12/97	02/03/98	Volunteer	16
LOVELOCK	Jno.	LM	278	21	London	25/12/98	02/03/98	Volunteer	14
LYNHAM	Patk.	LM	517	40	Dublin	06/04/98	06/04/98	Volunteer	26
	Also listed @ 3 in Supernumerary list								
MACKLEY	Heny	LM	162	20	London	26/09/97	07/01/98	VolunteerEnterprize	9
MACKLIN	Jas.	LM	367	27	Wallingfrd	12/02/98	04/03/98	Volunteer	19
MACKY	Hugh	PteRM	22			31/12/97	31/12/97	C.H.Q.	35
MAJOR	Simon	PteRM	70			04/01/98	04/01/98	C.H.Q.	36
	Killed in Action 01/08/98								
MALLETT	Humy.	AB	406	42	Plymouth	05/03/98	05/03/98	St. George	21
MARKIN	Patk.	PteRM	24			31/12/97	31/12/97	C.H.Q.	35
MARSDEN	Wm.	LM.	291	34	Holbeach	23/12/97	02/03/98		15

1	2	3	4	5	6	7	8	9	10
MARSHALL	Jno.	2nd Mate	73	40	Sunderland	25/11/97	01/01/98	Monmouth/Victory	4
MARSHALL	Wm. N.G.S.M.	AB	84	24	Edinburgh	25/11/97	01/01/98	Monmouth/Victory	5
MARTIN	Jno.	LM	299	20	Birmingham	25/12/97	02/03/98	Volunteer	15
MARTIN	Richard	Boy1st	1	17	Chatham	14/11/97	07/01/98	Volunteers1st Scipio/Zealand	31
	Killed in Action 01/08/98 Listed @1 on Boys 1st class								
MASON	Alex	AB	57	28	Aberdeen	25/11/97	01/01/98	Monmouth/Victory	3
MASTRASS	Jno. N.G.S.M.	Boy 2nd	5	18	Jersey	16/11/97	07/01/98	Scipio/Zealand	32
MAUGHER	Jas.	LM	372	20	County Carlow	13/02/98	04/03/98	Volunteer	19
MEALS	Jas.	LM	192	27	Dereham	13/04/97	07/01/98	Lincoln Substitute	10
MEANS	Chas.	AB To05/05/98 then S.Masters mate	49	28	Londonderry	25/11/97	01/01/98	Monmouth/Victory	3
MEEK	Timy.	Qtr Gnnr	441	31	Norwich	05/03/98	05/03/98	St. George	23
MELOY	Philip	PteRM	35			31/12/97	31/12/97	C.H.Q.	35
MELVIN	Jas.	AB To 01/05/98 then 2nd Mas.	459	29	Portsmth	05/03/98	05/03/98	St.George	23
MENTOR	Heny.	LM	281	21	Kent Goodnestown	21/09/97	02/03/98	Volunteer	15
MENZIES	Jas.	LM	204	27	Perthshire	24/04/97	07/01/98	Lincoln Substitute	11
MERCER	Wm.	PteRM	66			04/01/98	04/01/98	C.H.Q.	36
MEREDITH	Thos.	LM	375	24	County Meath	15/02/98	04/04/98		19

79

1	2	3	4	5	6	7	8	9	10
MIDDLETON	Josh. N.G.S.M.	PteRM	53			04/01/98	04/01/98	C.H.Q.	35
MILLIDON	Thos.	AB	232	34	Cornwall	07/11/97	07/01/98	Scipio Zealand	12
MILLS	Tim.	AB	44	34	London	25/11/97	01/01/98	Monmouth/Victory	3
MILLS	Thos.	LM	356	24	Edinburgh	01/02/98	04/03/98		18
MILTON	Thos.	PteRM	76			05/01/98	05/01/98	C.H.Q.	36
MONKS	Chas.	AB	421	30	Gloucester	05/03/98	05/03/98	St. George	22
MORRISON	Wm.	LM	311	28	Inniskilling	28/12/97	02/03/98	Volunteer	16
MOSS	Thos.	LM	369	23	Bolsham Cambridgeshire	12/02/98	04/03/98	Volunteer	19
MOXAM	Robt.	Boy3rd	6	16	London	16/11/97	07/01/98	Scipio Zealand	33
MULLIGAN	Patk.	PteRM				19/03/98	20/03/98	P.H.Q.	37
MUNDAN	Wm.	Ord	241	40	London	20/01/98	20/01/98	Haslar Hospital	13
MUNDRO	Pedro	AB	558	38	Malta	23/05/98	23/05/98		28
MUNNS	Wm.	AB	438	25	Yarmouth	05/03/98	05/03/98	St. George	22
	To 01/05/98 then Carpenter's Crew								
MURPHY	Peter	PteRM	36			31/12/97	31/12/97	C.H.Q.	35
MURPHY	Philip	LM	214	22	Cork	15/10/97	07/01/98	PrinceFrederick	11
MURPHY	Stephn.	AB	58	35	Ross Ireland	25/11/97	01/01/98	Monmouth/Victory	3
	Killed in Action 01/08/98								
MYERS	Edwd.	AB	435	47	Whitby	05/03/98	05/03/98	St. George	22
McARTHUR	Saml.	Ord	492	22	Inniskilling	05/03/98	05/03/98	St. George	25
McCLANAGHAN	Wm.	PteRM	58			04/01/98	04/01/98		35
McCLOAD	Roger	AB	50	30	Inverness	25/.11/97	01/01/98	Monmouth/Victory	3
	To 30/03/98 then Coxswain								

1	2	3	4	5	6	7	8	9	10
McCOY	Alexn.	AB	76	28	Tynmouth	25/11/97	01/01/98	Monmouth/Victory	4
		To 01/05/98 then Yeoman Sheets							
McERWIN	Jno	AB	48	25	Argyleshire	25/11/97	01/01/98	Monmouth/Victory	3
McGEE	Wm.	PteRM	13			31/12/97	31/12/97	C.H.Q.	34
McGINNIS	Arthr.	LM	321	27	Kildare	30/12/97	02/03/98	Volunteer	17
McKELVIE	Jas.	PteRM	20			31/12/97	31/12/97	C.H.Q.	34
McLAUGHLAN	Jas.	AB	59	24	London derry	25/11/97	01/01/98	Monmouth/Victory	3
McMAKEN	Jno.	PteRM	18			31/12/97	31/12/97	C.H.Q.	34
McNEIL	Jno.	LM	190	31	Bristol	13/04/97	07/01/98	Hull Substitute	10
McQUILLER	Jno.	PteRM	89			04/01/98	04/01/98	C.H.Q.	37
	Killed in Action 01/08/98								
McWILLIAMS	Geo.	AB	27	20	Dundee	13/07/97	01/01/98	Prest Monmouth	2
NAYLOR	Edward	LM	505	20	London	17/03/98	17/03/98	Volunteer	26
	N.G.S.M.	To 01/07/98 then AB Discharged 05/08/98 on promotion							
NEALE	Jno.	PteRM	71			04/01/98	04/01/98	C.H.Q.	36
NEALE	Lawc.	AB	457	28	County Of Carlow	05/03/98	05/03/98	St. George	23
NEAL	Thos.	AB	398	30	Dungawon	05/03/98	05/03/98	St. George	20
NELSON.KB	Horatio Rear Admiral of the Blue					28/03/98	28/03/98		39
NETTLESHIP	Wm.	LM	378	23	London	15/02/98	04/03/98	Volunteer	19
NEWLAND	Dennis	AB	230	46	Dublin	16/11/97	07/01/98	Scipio Zealand	12
NICHOLS	Jas.	AB	85	24	Plymouth	01/01/98	01/01/98	St. George	5
	Killed in Action 01/08/98								
NOBLE	Chris.	Lieut.RM	1			31/12/97	31/12/97	C.H.Q.	34

1	2	3	4	5	6	7	8	9	10
NOOKE	Jno.	AB	126	26	London	01/01/98	01/01/98	St. George	7
		To 01/05/98 then Armourer's Mate							
NORTON	Thos.	PteRM	32			31/12/97	31/12/97	C.H.Q.	35
NOWLAND	Jas.	LM	353	22	Ireland	31/01/98	04/03/98	Volunteer	18
OAGEN	Danl.	AB	70	40	Tipperary	25/11/97	01/01/98	Monmouth/Victory	4
OFFICE	Josa. N.G.S.M.	PteRM	10			31/12/97	31/12/97	C.H.Q.	34
ONION	Jas.	AB	254	22	London	14/02/98	14/02/98	Volunteer	13
		To 30/03/98 then Armourer's Mate							
ORGAN	Jas.	AB	405	40	London	05/03/98	05/03/98	St. George	21
OSBORNE	Saml. N.G.S.M.	Ord	482	22	London	05/03/98	05/03/98	St. George	25
PAGE	Wm. N.G.S.M.	AB	448	22	Yarmouth	05/03/98	05/03/98	St. George	23
PALMER	Saml.	AB	446	25	Hads Norfolk	05/03/98	05/03/98	St. George	23
PARISH	Jno.	Ord	521	22	Surrey	06/04/98	06/04/98	Prest Diadem	27
	Killed in Action 01/08/98								
PARK	Chas.	LM	288	20	Norwich	15/12/97	02/03/98	Volunteer	15
PARKER	Thos.	LM	340	26	Cork	04/02/98	02/03/98	Volunteer	17
PARKINSON *	W.S.	Lieut Commission 20/12/97	1			20/12/97	24/12/97		1
PARSONS	Wm.	LM	235	36	Bristol	16/11/97	07/01/98	Scipio Zealand	12
PARTRIDGE	Shakepr.	LM	287	20	Sharnham Norfolk	12/12/97	02/03/98	Volunteer	15

1	2	3	4	5	6	7	8	9	10
PATTEN	Arch.	Masters	28			25/11/97	05/01/98	Victory	2
		Mate to 07/01/98 then Midshipman Discharged August 98 to *Majestic*							
PEACOCK	Willm.	AB	140	27	Bristol	01/01/98	01/01/98	St. George	7
		To 20/04/98 then Midshipman							
PEAKE	Saml.	AB	442	40	Yarmouth	05/03/98	05/03/98	St. George	23
		To 01/05/98 then Qtr Gnnr							
PEDWIN	Wm.	AB	91	23	Falmouth	01/01/98	01/01/98	St. George	5
PEMBERTON	Chas.	Armourer	34	37	Chester	25/11/97	01/01/98		2
PEMBERTON	Jno.	Boy 3rd	17	12	Portsmouth	01/05/98	01/05/98		33
PENN	Thos.	Ord.	26	20	Chatham	29/12/97	29/12/97		2
		To 01/07/98 then Midshipman							
PENNY	Wm.	AB	424	40	Bristol	05/03/98	05/03/98	St. George	22
PEPPERKORN	Wm.	Sgt.RM	50			04/01/98	04/01/98	C.H.Q.	35
PETERS	Jno.	Ord	486	21	Bombay	05/03/98	05/03/98	St. George	25
PETTES	Thos.	AB	466	22	Folkstone	05/03/98	05/03/98	St. George	24
PINHAM	Saml.	AB	137	66	Salisbury	01/01/98	01/01/98	St. George	7
PIPS	Chas.	LM	183	20	London	08/10/97	07/01/98	Rosario	10
PLAFORD	Thos.	AB	503	23	Norwich	05/03/98	10/03/98	St. George	26
		To 30/03/98 then Midshipman							
PLANT	Saml.	SgtRM				31/12/97	31/12/97	C.H.Q.	34
PLOWMAN	Chas.	LM	345	20	Monmouth Shire	27/01/98	04/03/98	Volunteer	18
POLISE	Jemera	AB	554	23	Malta	19/04/98	19/04/98		28
POOLE	Danl.	AB	410	32	Bristol	05/03/98	05/03/98	St. George	21
		To 01/05/98 then Yeoman of Sheets							

83

1	2	3	4	5	6	7	8	9	10
POPEE	Robt.	LM	179	20	Suffolk	04/10/97	07/01/98	VolunteerEnterprize	9
PORTAN	Jno.	Boy 3rd	15	15	Deptford	07/02/98	07/02/98	Volunteer	33
		N.G.S.M. (as John Porter Greenwich Hospital number 8672)							
POTTS	Jno.	AB	31	47	Durham Hartlepool	25/11/97	01/01/98		2
POTTS	John	AB	142	30	Plymouth Dock	01/01/98	01/01/98	St. George	8
POWELL	Thos.	Boy 3rd	16	19	Portsmouth	30/03/98	30/03/98		33
POWER	Nichs.	AB	408	35	County Wexford	05/03/98	05/03/98	St. George	21
PRICE	Wm.	LM	200	20	Railey	15/04/97	07/01/98	Lincoln substitute	10
PRICE(2nd)	Wm.	Ord	484	22	London	05/03/98	05/03/98	St. George	25
PROBY	Granville	Boy1st	6			21/03/98	21/03/98	Volunteer	31
PULLEN	Jno.	AB	43	37	London	25/11/97	01/01/98	Monmouth/Victory	3
PUTLAND	Jno.	Mid	252			01/02/98	10/02/98	Derris pay list	13
QUICK	Jas.	Coxswain	502	35	Plymouth	06/03/98	10/03/98	Zealand St.George	26
		To 30/03/98 then Midshipman							
QUINN	Edwd.	AB	393	28	Dublin	05/03/98	05/03/98	St. George	20
RAMSEY	Thomas	Cook	145	31	North Barack	13/12/97	03/01/98		8
		Officer's Warrant 13/12/97							
RANDALL	Thos.	LM	206	20	Dorchestr	08/10/97	07/01/98	Rosario	11
RANDALL	Wm.	AB	131	26	Plymouth	01/01/98	01/01/98	St. George	7
RAZIEUR	Josh.	AB	471	23	Genoa	05/03/98	05/03/98	St. George	24
REARDON	Jno.	LM	196	28	Kilmarnock	15/04/97	07/01/98	Lincoln substitute	10
REED	Danl.	LM	341	20	Fifeshire	18/12/97	02/03/98	late Wolf	18

1	2	3	4	5	6	7	8	9	10
REES	Jno.	Sailmaker Warrant 15/01/98	222	40	Pembrokeshire	07/11/97	07/01/98	Ruby	12
REGISTER	Wm.	LM	382	32	Norfolk Salters load	02/02/98	04/03/98	Volunteer	20
RETALLICK	Saml.	AB	136	26	Helstone	01/01/98	01/01/98	St. George	7
REYNOLDS	Jas.	PteRM N.G.S.M. (Greenwich Hospital No. 9305)	101			19/03/98	20/03/98	P.H.Q.	38
RICE	Mark	PteRM				04/01/98	04/01/98	C.H.Q.	36
RICHARDS	Evan	AB	418	22	Glamorganshire	05/03/98	05/03/98	St. George	21
RICHARDSON	Jno.	AB To 05/05/98 then Yeoman of the Sheets	42	35	Newcastle	25/11/97	01/01/98	Monmouth/Victory	3
RIDING	Murphy	AB	231	37	Cork	16/11/97	07/01/98	Scipio Zealand	12
ROACH	Jas.	PteRM				31/12/97	31/12/97	C.H.Q.	35
ROBERT	Edward	PteRM	25			31/12/97	31/12/97	C.H.Q.	35
ROBERTS	Spry	AB	113	24	Saltash	01/01/98	01/01/98	St. George	6
ROBERTSON	Jas.	AB	429	27	Bristol	05/03/98	05/03/98	St. George	22
ROGERS	Jerh.	PteRM	77			04/01/98	04/01/98	C.H.Q.	36
RUBBRO	Jos.	LM	322	22	Northampton	30/12/97	02/03/98	Volunteer	17
RUMSEY	Saml.	AB	112	41	Wiltshire	01/01/98	01/01/98	St.George	6
RUSSEL	Philip	Ord	526	24	Cork	19/04/98	19/04/98	Prest Diadem	27
RYAN	Jas.	Ord	270	22	Limerick	12/2/98	02/03/98	Substitute	14
SAGE	Jas.	AB To 01/05/98 then Qtr Gunner	139	27	Bristol	01/01/98	01/01/98	St. George	7
SAMUEL	Isaac	LM	178	22	Chatham	04/10/97	07/01/98	VolunteerEnterprize	9

1	2	3	4	5	6	7	8	9	10
SANDY	Willm.	Ord	261	29	Galway	24/02/98	24/02/98	In lieu Jno.White	14
SAUL	Richd.	Mid	32			25/11/97	01/01/98		2
SAWYER	Jas.	LM	303	26	Lowestoft	03/12/97	02/03/98	Volunteer	16
		To 01/05/98 then Ships Corpl.							
SAY	Saml.	AB	449	49	Norwich	05/03/98	05/03/98	St. George	23
SAYER	Benjn.	LM	342	20	Norwich	05/12/97	02/03/98	Volunteer	18
SCOSSA	Fras.	Pilot				20/06/98	20/06/98		43
		From Faro of Messina - discharged 19/07/98 at Syracuse							
SCOTT	Robt.	PteRM				04/01/98	04/01/98	C.H.Q.	36
SCOTT	Wm.	AB	106	40	Glasgow	01/01/98	01/01/98	St. George	6
SEARLE	Rich.	AB	132	24	Torquay	01/01/98	01/01/98	St. George	7
		To 01/07/98 then Qtr Mas.							
SEPORT	Charatus	AB	548	25	Malta	19/04/98	19/04/98		28
SEYMOUR	Thos.	Mid	510			23/03/98	23/03/98	Irresistable	26
	Killed in Action 01/08/98								
SHANNON	Jno.	LM	373	22	Prussia	14/02/98	04/03/98	Volunteer	19
					Lent to *La Fortune* 12/08/98				
SHEEN	Morris	LM	195	40	Cork	13/04/97	07/01/98	Lincoln Substitute	10
SHIPPARD	Alex.	Purser	4			24/12/97	24/12/97		1
SHIRLEY	Geo.	AB	401	25	London	05/03/98	05/03/98	St. George	21
N.G.S.M.		To 01/07/98 then Qtr Masters Mate							
SHORT	Patk.	PteRM	43			31/12/97	31/12/97	C.H.Q.	35
SIMMS	Robert	AB	141	22	Bridport	01/01/98	01/01/98	St. George	8
		To 01/05/98 then Qtr Gunner							
SIMPSON	Robt.	PteRM	64			04/01/98	04/01/98	C.H.Q.	36

1	2	3	4	5	6	7	8	9	10
SKINNER	Jno.	LM	325	24	Dorking Surrey	01/01/98	02/03/98	Volunteer	17
SLATER	Rheun.	AB	54	27	Guernsey	25/11/97	01/01/98	Monmouth/Victory	3
SMIT	Eyridie	LM				11/06/98	11/06/98		42
		Shown on Supernumary list H.Courier of Cadiz prize from *Alexander*							
SMITH(2)	Denis	LM	334	21	Yarmouth	03/01/98	02/03/98	Volunteer	17
SMITH	Geo.	PteRM	38			31/12/98	31/12/98	C.H.Q.	35
SMITH	Henry	Drummer RM	68			04/01/98	04/01/98	C.H.Q.	35
SMITH	Isaac	AB	68	25	Poole	25/11/98	01/01/98	Monmouth/Victory	4
SMITH	Jas.	AB	125	27	London	01/01/98	01/01/98	St. George	7
SMITH	Jas.	PteRM	46			31/12/97	31/12/97	C.H.Q.	35
SMITH	Saml.	AB	453	29	Suffolk Kessingland	05/03/98	05/03/98	St. George	23
SMITH	Sm.	Boy3rd	8	19	America	16/11/97	07/01/98	Scipio Zealand	33
	Killed in action 01/08/98 Listed on Boy's muster								
SMITH	Thos.	AB	422	35	Bristol	05/03/98	05/03/98	St. George	22
SMITH(1)	Wm.	LM	205	27	N.Shields	08/10/97	07/01/98	Rosario	11
SPEED	Wm.	AB	414	22	Bristol	05/03/98	05/03/98	St. George	21
SPENCER	Michl.	Masters Mate	29			25/11/97	01/01/98	Victory	2
SPENCER	Mundy	PteRM	21			31/12/97	31/12/07	C.H.Q.	35
SPENCER	Thos.	AB	238	27	Nottingham	13/01/98	13/01/98		12
		Admiral's retinue shown discharged 28/03/98 and entered 29/03/98							39
SPOONER	Jno.	LM	208	20	London	08/10/97	07/01/98	Rosario	11

87

1	2	3	4	5	6	7	8	9	10
SPRINGALD	Geo.	Ord	228	27	Norwich	16/11/97	07/01/98	Scipio Zealand	12
SPROULL	Jas.	3rdMate	262			23/02/98	26/02/98		14
		To 1st May then 2nd Mate - Warrant 23/01/98							
STACEY	Wm.	Ord	495	20	Somerset	05/03/98	05/03/98	St. George	25
STAIDES	Jas.	Boy3rd	7	16	Pinner	16/11/97	07/01/98	Scipio Zealand	33
STEVENS	Wm.	Ord	274	32	Uxbridge	22/02/98	02/03/98	Prest	14
STROLGER	Edmd.	AB	444	20	Lowestoft	05/03/98	05/03/98	St.George	23
STUBBS	Jno.	LM	174	24	Ashburn	03/10/97	07/01/98	Volunteer Enterprize	9
STUBBS	Philip	AB	118	23	Devon Modbury	01/01/98	01/01/98	St. George	6
STURGEON	Roger	PteRM	74			04/01/98	04/01/98	C.H.Q.	36
STYLES	Jno.	CorpRM	51			04/01/98	04/01/98	C.H.Q.	35
		To 08/05/98 then Pte to 26/05/98 then Corp.							
SULLIVAN N.G.S.M.	Michl.	AB	109	43	Plymouth Dock	01/01/98 Discharged 04/01/98	01/01/98	St. George	6
SULLIVAN	John	AB	419	45	Tralee Ireland	05/03/98	05/03/98	St. George	21
SULLIVAN	Owen	AB	95	41	Plymouth Dock	01/01/98	01/01/98	St. George	5
SUNAM	Js. **Killed in Action 01/08/98**	LM	307	30	Kings	27/12/97	02/03/98	Volunteer	16
SWELL	Heny. **Killed in Action 01/08/98**	Ord	519	35	London	06/04/98	06/04/98	San Damaso	26
SWINEY	Jno.	LM	202	39	County Waterford	15/04/97	07/01/98	Lincoln Substitute	11

1	2	3	4	5	6	7	8	9	10
SWINEY	Valentine	LM	335	21	Dublin	03/01/98	02/03/98	Volunteer	17
TAYLOR(1ST)	Jas.	AB	93	36	Plymouth	01/01/98	01/01/98	St. George	5
TAYLOR	Jas.	AB	509	20	London	22/03/98	22/03/98	Volunteer	26
TAYLOR	Jno.G.	Boy1st	5			10/02/98	10/02/98	Volunteer	31
	Died 03/08/98 of Wounds received in Action								
TAYLOR	Jno.	Boy3rd	3	13	Plymouth	01/01/98	01/01/98	St. George	33
TAYLOR(1ST)	Richd.	LM	370	23	Hertford Shire	12/02/98	04/03/98	Volunteer	19
THOMAS(1ST)	Geo.	AB	143	24	Newcastle	01/01/98	01/01/98	St. George	8
	To 01/05/98 then Qtr Master's Mate								
THOMAS	Jno.	LM	312	20	Newbury	29/12/97	02/03/98	Volunteer	16
THOMAS	Thos.	LM	371	34	Richmond	13/02/98	04/03/98	Volunteer	19
THOMPSON	Geo.	LM	217	24	London	26/10/97	07/01/98	Grana with ticket Late Sandwich	11
THOMPSON	Jno.	Ord	264	20	Boston	01/02/98	02/03/98	Zealand Prest	14
THOMPSON	Richd.	LM	332	20	Altrincham	30/01/98	02/03/98	Volunteer	17
THOMPSON	Wm.	LM	290	20	Lanarkshire	20/12/97	02/03/98	Volunteer	15
THORNE	Josh.	AB	426	26	Stoway Somersetshire	05/03/98	05/03/98	St. George	22
THORNLEY	Jas.	Ord	275	26	Liverpool	23/02/98	02/03/98	Volunteer	14
THURLING	Benj.	LM	166	30	Hingham Norfolk	29/09/97	07/01/98	VolunteerEnterprize	9
TIERNEY	Jas.	CorpRM	4			31/12/97	31/12/97	C.H.Q.	34
	To 01/07/98 then Private								

1	2	3	4	5	6	7	8	9	10
TIPPETT	Jn.	Qtr.Gnnr	133	48	Helston Cornwall	01/01/98	01/01/98	St. George	7
THOMPSON(1st)	Jno.	LM	160	21	Barkswell Warwickshire	23/09/97	07/01/98	Enterprize	8
TOOTHACRE	Thos.	LM	305	23	London	04/12/97	02/03/98	Volunteer	16
TOYNTON	Davd.	LM	376	20	Sutton Lincolnshire	15/02/98	04/03/98	Volunteer	19
TRIPP	Jno.	AB	451	25	Yarmouth	05/03/98	05/03/98	St. George	23
TRIPP	Robt.	AB	462	26	Yarmouth	05/03/98	05/03/98	St. George	24
TRUE	Saml.	LM	328	21	London	28/12/97	02/03/98	Volunteer	17
TURNER	Chas.	LM	247	23	Oxford	02/02/98	02/02/98	Volunteer	13
VANSTOKEN	Peter	PteRM	62			04/01/98	04/01/98	C.H.Q.	36
VASSALL	Dora	AB	551	30	Malta	19/04/98	19/04/98		28
VASSALL	Nathl.	Lieut	148			20/12/97	07/01/98		8
		Commission 20/12/97 Named as wounded in the official dispatch							
VELLA	Jemera	AB	556	30	Malta	30/04/98	30/04/98		28
VELLA	Salvo	AB	555	22	Malta	30/04/98	30/04/98		28
WAGSTAFF	Wm.	LM	301	22	Coventry	17/12/97	02/03/98	Volunteer	16
WALDEN	Thos.	AB	105	39	Penton	01/01/98	01/01/98	St. George	6
		To 01/05/98 then 2nd Gunner							
WALLER	Wm.	AB	81	22	Stockton	25/11/97	01/01/98	Monmouth/Victory	5
	Killed in Action 01/08/98								
WALSH	Philip	AB	390	28	Dublin	05/03/98	05/03/98	St. George	20
WAREY	Willm.	AB	123	25	Looe Cornwall	01/01/98	01/01/98	St. George	7

1	2	3	4	5	6	7	8	9	10
WARD	Jno.	PteRM	95			19/03/98	20/03/98	P.H.Q.	37
WARNE	Wm.	AB	134	21	St.Asaph	01/01/98	01/01/98	St. George	7
WARREN	Jno.	AB	51	25	Yarmouth	25/11/97	01/01/98	Monmouth/Victory	3
WATERS	Wm.	AB	41	26	Uxbridge	25/11/97	01/01/98	Monmouth/Victory	3
WATTS	Robt.	LM	337	21	Norwich	04/12/97	02/03/98	Volunteer	17
WEATHERSTONE*	Jno.	Mid	239			19/01/98	19/01/98		12
	N.G.S.M.	To 25/02/98 then Master's Mate Listed as wounded in the official dispatch							
WEEKS	Jno.	PteRM	60			04/01/98	04/01/98	C.H.Q.	35
WEIR	Saml.	Ord	257	20	Bristol	15/02/98	15/02/98		13
		From 2nd Class Boy							
WELLS	Wm.	LM	286	20	Holworth	12/12/97	02/03/98	Volunteer	15
					Suffolk	Lent to *La Fortune* privateer 12/08/98			
WEST	Edward	Mid	513			30/03/98	30/03/98	Neptune	26
WESTICOTT	Jno.	Master at Arms	242	30	Plymouth	20/01/98	20/01/98		13
		Warrant 12/01/98							
WHEATLY	Geo.	PteRM	90			04/01/98	04/01/98	C.H.Q.	37
	Killed in Action 01/08/98								
WHEELER	Jno.	LM	279	20	Chipping Ongar	25/12/97	02/03/98	Volunteer	14
WHELER	Martin	AB	77	38	Waterford	25/11/97	01/01/98		4
	Killed in Action 01/08/98								
WHITE(2nd)	Jno.	LM	318	24	London	30/12/97	02/03/98	Volunteer	16
WIBBER	Philip	LM	348	23	Bethnal Green	29/01/98	04/03/98	Volunteer	18
WILCOX	Wm.	LM	216	26	Harlow	15/10/97	07/01/98	Prince Frederick	11
	Died 08/08/98 of Wounds received in Action								

91

1	2	3	4	5	6	7	8	9	10
WILKINS	Wm.	Ord	498	38	Romsey	05/03/98	05/03/98	St. George	25
WILLCOCKS	Robt.	AB	399	38	Devonshire	05/03/98	05/03/98	St. George	20
WILLIAMS	Edmd.	PteRM	29			31/12/97	31/12/97	C.H.Q.	35
WILLIAMS	Jno.	AB	127	30	London	01/01/98	01/01/98	St. George	7
WILLIAMS(2nd)	Jno.	AB	428	25	Cork	05/03/98	05/03/98	St. George	22
WILLIAMS	Thos.	PteRM	94			19/03/98	20/03/98	P.H.Q	37
WILLIS	Fras.	AB	423	46	Bristol	05/03/98	05/03/98	St. George	22
WILSON	Arthur	Caulker	500	21	Manchester	05/03/98	05/03/98	Zealand Volunteer	25
WILSON	John	AB	445	23	Yarmouth	05/03/98	05/03/98	St. George	23
WILSON	Mark	AB	66	27	Hull	25/11/97	01/01/98	Monmouth/Victory	4
WILSTED	Jas.	LM	331	24	London	03/01/98	02/03/98	Volunteer	17
WISHT	Saml.	LM		from 2/3 allowance list		29/06/98	29/06/98		42
WITCHER	Henry	LM	215	31	White Parish, Wiltshire	15/10/97	07/01/98	Prince Frederick	11
WOOD	Heny.	LM	317	27	London	30/12/97	02/03/98	Volunteer	16
WOODIN	Jno.	Mid	560	21		14/08/98	14/08/98	La Mutine	28
WOODWARD	Jas.	AB	434	25	Gloucester	05/03/98	05/03/98	St. George	22
	To 01/03/98 then Carpenter's Crew								
	Killed in Action 01/08/98								
WOOLCOX	Geo.	LM	153	20	Leicester	28/09/97	07/01/98	Volunteer Enterprize	8
WOOLFORD	Wm.	LM	324	22	London	01/01/98	02/03/98	Volunteer	17
WRIGHT	Chas.	LM	329	20	London	28/12/97	02/03/98	Volunteer	17
WRIGHT	Jas.	Ord	531	23	Middlesex	19/04/98	19/04/98	Volunteer	27
	Died 03/08/98 of wounds received in Action								
WRIGHT	Jno.	PteRM	98			19/03/98	20/03/98	P.H.Q.	37

1	2	3	4	5	6	7	8	9	10
WRIGHT	Jno.	Ord	276	23	London	23/02/98	02/03/98	Prest	14
YAXLEY	Saml.	AB	450	23	Norwich	05/03/98	05/03/98	St. George	23
YOUNG	Thos.	LieutRM	48			04/01/98	04/01/98	C.H.Q.	35
ZAMOUT	Joseppe	AB	543	42	Malta	19/04/98	19/04/98		28

'Landsman', National Maritime Museum, London.

Footnotes of Interest concerning the Muster List

Readers may notice the absence of some of the sequential numbers in the Muster List as published. As the booklet is timed to coincide with the bi-centenary of the Battle of the Nile, those individuals not present at the Battle have been omitted. A couple of exceptions are Hardy and Scossa, the former because of his unique place in the Nelson history, and the latter out of interest in the role he performed in the hunt for the French fleet. An example of the omissions is the deserters.

Deserters

No. 55 was allotted to a Geo. Smith who 'R' (Ran) at Portsmouth on 10/04/98, and the desertions chart some of the progress of the Vanguard i.e.: -

At Chatham	10/01/98 1 deserter – 24/01/98 3 deserters – 29/01/98 2 deserters
At Sheerness	02/03/98 3 deserters – 03/03/98 1 deserter – 04/03/98 2 deserters – 09/03/98 1 deserter
At Portsmouth	15/03/98 4 deserters – 16/03/98 2 deserters – 18/03/98 2 deserters –20/03/98 1 deserter
	27/03/98 5 deserters – 29/03/98 1 deserter - 08/04/98 2 deserters – 10/04/98 2 deserters
At Gibraltar	05/05/98 1 deserter – 08/05/98 1 deserter
At Syracuse	25/07/98 1 deserter

Discharged Sick
Losses through sickness have also been omitted and there are frequent references to discharges onto Hospital ships – *Union, Argonaut* and to Haslar Hospital, prompting the following letter for reserves:-
TO EVAN NEAPEAN, ESQ., SECRETARY TO THE ADMIRALTY.

[Original, in the Admiralty. At 8pm on 29 March, Rear-Admiral Sir Horatio Nelson hoisted his Flag, Blue at the Mizen, on board the *Vanguard*, at Spithead. After remaining for some days at St. Helen's, she quitted England, on 10 April, with the Portugal, Gibraltar, and Mediterranean convoy to join Lord St. Vincent's Fleet at Lisbon]

Sir   Vanguard, Spithead, 29 March, 1798. Wind N.N.E.
There being twenty-five men at the Hospital, who cannot return to the Ship before she proceeds to sea, nor can they be 'D.S.Q.', they not having been twenty-eight days at the Hospital, and also five or six men absent without leave, who cannot be 'Run' on the Ship's Books, not having been absent three musters; therefore I beg leave to observe that after the Ship has been a few days at sea she will be considerably short of complement. I have therefore to request that their Lordships will be pleased to order the same number as will be left ashore, in order that she may sail with her number complete.
                    I am, Sir, &c.
                    HORATIO NELSON

Manning the Ship

The sequence of manning the ship as shown by the dates of 'Appearance' on board follow a logical progression, indicating initially an establishment for control rather than sailing, i.e.-between Sept/Dec, 1797:

Captain
Lieutenants (3)
Master
Purser
Surgeon and Surgeon's Mate
Carpenters Crew (1)
Clerk (1)   Cook (1)
Ordinary Seaman (1)   Landsmen (3)
Lieutenant RM Sergeant RM (3) Corporal RM (2) Privates RM (26)

Large batches of seamen arrived during the next few months – 155 on 1 Jan 1798 239 on 2 March 1798. and in early April, perhaps in response to the above letter, a further 43.

The Muster Table (page 57) showing the summary of the ship's complement includes the heading: -
Vanguard Complement 590 Men to 28 March, 1798 then 595 Men'.
And separately listed on page 39 is 'Rear Admiral Sir Horatio Nelson K.B. Secretary and Retinue' ie. Campbell, Secretary and ABs Spencer, Allen and Leary'.
Captain Berry must have been very relieved to finally sail in early April, 1798!

Prisoners at 2/3 Allowance of Provisions
Page 44 of the Muster records nine prisoners carried briefly during the period of the summary. Listed as 'Appearing' on 2nd July 1798 are Fras. Gisines, Felix Herke, Carloe Agnes, Domino Frimo, Andres Dogne, Juan Monte, Thos. Girschell who were discharged on 25 July, 1798 at Syracuse.
A Michl. Sequi and Jean Baptisto are listed as having been taken off the wreck of the French Ships.

Temporary Chaplain
Another short entry on the muster list was Reverend Geo. Huddersford, Chaplain who was 'Entered' in the muster on the 3rd Feb., 'Appeared' on the 14th Feb., and was discharged on 17 March 1798 'By request.' Whatever lay behind his brief tenure the Rev. Comyn arrived within a week and became an indelible part of the history of the ship during a momentous year.

Death in the course of duty
The muster records a sequence of discharges through illness to hospital ships and more tragically the loss of life through accidents: -
21/05/98 Mick Midshipman and Neale AB aged 23yrs from Ireland - Accident on board
25/05/98 Westcott AB aged 23yrs from Chudleigh, Devon - fell overboard and drowned
19/07/98 Anthony AB aged 22yrs from South Wales - fell overboard and drowned

Rank/Rates
Rough totals of the grades for seamen show Landsmen 174; Ordinary 51; Able Seamen 198
With the inclusion of Boys ages range from 13 to 66 years of age with an average for seamen of 29 years.

Possible family links amongst the crew
From the surnames, ages and place of birth, where shown, there appear to be a number of brothers amongst the crew. Sadly Captain Faddy of the Marines was one of those killed in the action on 1st August and Captain Berry had taken on board Midshipman Faddy as one of his young protégés.

United Nations of sailors
Reviewing their places of birth, as listed, the crew came from as far apart as New York and Bombay, Prussia and Quebec, with significant numbers from Malta, a batch of 20 ABs of Maltese descent appearing on board on 19th April, 1798.

'Widows' men'
Six 'widows' men' (numbers 7-12 inclusive) were listed, in accordance with approved practice, to be borne at able seamen's wages which were assigned to the fund for paying officers' widows' pensions.

CHAPTER 5

THE AFTERMATH

The second day of the Battle, on the 2nd August, 1798, after fighting finally subsided, was spent collecting prisoners from rafts and floating wreckage until finally some two thousand unwounded and fifteen hundred wounded were collected. Nelson sent a memorandum to his captains, "Almighty God having blessed His Majesty's Arms with Victory, the Admiral intends returning Public Thanksgiving for the same at two o'clock this day, and he recommends every Ship doing the same as soon as convenient." The French officers from the 'citizens navy' held prisoner, expressed their surprise and admiration at the discipline, which had enforced attendance at the services; Napoleon having proscribed the practice of religion earlier in the Revolution. The same evening Nelson was host to dinner in his cabin with wounded French officers.

The Battle was a triumph for Nelson and his squadron, being the first large-scale reverse suffered by the French since the war opened. It was all the more remarkable as the French fleet was superior in men and armaments, had chosen the position against the shallows, were protected by shore batteries, and could concentrate on handling their guns. They were overwhelmed by the initiative and skill of Nelson's captains and the intensity and accuracy of British gunfire under the leadership of an inspired commander.

Whilst Napoleon had conquered Egypt, his army could never return home except by permission of the English fleet. Captain Berry was entrusted to carry Nelson's dispatches in the *Leander*, but *Le Gènèreux* off Crete intercepted them and he did not reach London until the last week of November 1798. However as was the usual practice a duplicate dispatch, carried in this case by acting Captain, Lieutenant Capel, with Lieutenant William Hoste taking passage, arrived at Naples on the *Mutine* and, when the victory was announced throughout Europe, every country but France rang with jubilation.

Aftermath of the Battle - The French perspective
A measure of the shock felt by the French may be gathered from intercepted correspondence from ControllerGeneral Poussielgue, the financial administrator of the Army of Egypt, who described the battle from his viewpoint on the top of houses ashore. He said 'the fatal engagement ruined all our hopes, it prevented us receiving the remainder of our forces, it left the field free for the English, rekindled the heart of the Emperor of Austria, opened the Mediterranean to the Russians and planted them on our frontiers'. Writing years later at St. Helena, Napoleon said, "If it had not been for the English, I should have been Emperor of the East, but wherever there is water to float a ship we are sure to find you in our way. I should have reached Constantinople and India, I should have changed the face of the world".

For the French navy the defeat was a disaster in terms of ships, men and morale. Bonaparte tried to play down the impact but knew his army could not return to France as there was no naval force left to protect the transports. The victory encouraged the Sultan to declare a holy war against the French and this forced Napoleon to march into Syria and besiege Acre where he "missed his destiny". The captured French naval personnel were well treated by the British but blamed by Bonaparte. It was easy for him to blame the dead de Brueys. He also accused Rear Admiral Blanquet of cowardice and hounded him so much that on his release from imprisonment in England the wounded Blanquet felt obliged to resign from the navy within a year. The ships which escaped from the Nile were subsequently captured and the victory encouraged the European powers to form a second coalition against France. As Bonaparte subsequently wrote: - "The loss of the battle of Aboukir had great influence on the affairs of Egypt and even on those of the world".

Sailors at Prayer led by Rev. S. Comyn
National Maritime Museum, London.

The REWARD of COURAGE, or NELSON TRIUMPHANT.

*The Valiant Nelson receiving the Trophy of victory from the second French Admiral –
May the contemplation of this subject inspire every British Heart with
loyalty and courage, and strike Dismay and Terror to those Enemies who will
arrogantly dare to cope with our Tar on the Ocean.
'Twas sacred Liberty the Hero fir'd
And struck the Blow, which won'dring Worlds admir'd.*

Warwick Leadlay Gallery

102

CHAPTER 6

RECEPTION OF THE VICTOR

The Honourable Captain Capel of the *Mutine* accompanied by his intended replacement, Lt. William Hoste delivered the letter from their commander to Sir William Hamilton, setting in train a sequence of events which were to detain Nelson in Italy for two years. Lady Hamilton was reported to have collapsed on hearing the news of the battle but revived promptly to sweep up the two messengers and carry them triumphantly in her carriage to spread the news to the populace. Emma penned an effusive letter to Nelson which Captain Hoste carried with him on his return with other correspondence for his commander; Captain Capel having left Naples for London.

Vanguard limped and was towed the 1300 miles to Italy to be welcomed, off Capri on 22 September 1798, by a flotilla including the King of Naples and the Hamiltons. Writing later to his wife Nelson described his welcome : -

> "Alongside my honoured friends came; the scene in the boat appeared terribly affecting. Up flew her ladyship and exclaiming: Oh God, is it possible! Fell into my arm more dead than alive. Tears, however, soon put matters to rights, when alongside came the King. He took me by the hand, calling me his deliverer and preserver with every other expression of kindness ... I hope one day to have the pleasure of introducing you to Lady Hamilton. She is one of the very best women in the world. How few could have made the turn she has. She is an honour to her sex and proof the even reputation may be regained but I own it requires a great soul".

Intending only to get *Vanguard* into shape, Nelson wrote to Earl St. Vincent declaring, "It is a country of fiddlers and poets, whores and scoundrels". But a whirl of events captured Nelson in a gilded web from which

Lady Hamilton welcoming the victors of the Nile   *Robert Hollingford*

Lady Hamilton by Schmidt
Reputedly Nelson's favourite picture and hung in his cabin

he found it difficult to extricate himself. Invited ashore, he stayed with the Hamiltons. He was feted and flattered, and soon became enmeshed in affairs which reflected little credit on his judgement. Following the discomforts he had experienced in the winter of 1797, recovering from the amputation and fretting about his future, it was a remarkable period in his life. The reports concerning the Battle prompted numerous personal, ministerial and royal tributes, which added to the glow from his victory, to the adulation and affection lavished on him, not least by the vibrant Emma Hamilton. The mercurial changes during the following years are part of another story but the influence played by *Vanguard*, with Nelson leading the squadron, changed the pattern of French domination although there were still land and sea battles to be endured before Bonaparte was finally ousted.

Unique gifts for a Hero
No present sent to Nelson after the Battle was so extraordinary as that which he received from his gallant friend, Captain Hallowell of the *Swiftsure*; and the idea could have occurred only to an original mind. After *L'Orient* blew-up, part of her mainmast was taken on board of the *Swiftsure*; and in May 1799, Captain Hallowell, fearing the effect of all the praise and flattery lavished on his Chief, determined to remind him that he was mortal. He therefore ordered a coffin to be made out of part of the *L'Orient's* mast, and was so careful

that nothing whatever should be used in its construction that was not taken from it. That the staples were formed of the spikes drawn from the cheeks of the mast, which were driven into the edge of the coffin, and when the lid was put on toggles were put into the staples to keep it down, so as to prevent the necessity of using nails or screws for that purpose. The nails of the coffin were likewise made from the spikes taken from the mast. A paper was pasted on the bottom, containing the following certificate: -

> "I do hereby certify that every part of this Coffin is made of the wood and iron of *L'Orient*, most of which was picked up by his Majesty's Ship, under my command, in the Bay of Aboukir. *Swiftsure* May 23, 1799
>
> Ben. Hallowell"

The following letter accompanied this singular present.

> THE RIGHT HON. LORD NELSON K.B.
>
> "My Lord
> Herewith I send you a Coffin made of part of *L'Orient's* Mainmast, that when you are tired of this Life you may be buried in one of your own Trophies – but may that period be far distant, is the sincere wish of your obedient and much obliged servant.
> *Swiftsure*, August 23rd, 1798   BEN. HALLOWELL

The astonishment that prevailed among the crew of the *Vanguard*, Lord Nelson's flagship was long remembered. It is satisfactory to state that Nelson was actually buried in this coffin.

Sword from the Egyptian Club
The Captains who formed the Egyptian Club in due time presented Lord Nelson with a sword in tribute and to mark their joint achievement at the Nile. Specially commissioned the pommel was in the form of the head of a crocodile; the grip in the body of a crocodile; displaying Nelson's arms and figures of Britannia and Africa. The Guard displayed an enamel of battle scenes. The sword was not to survive intact, the blade being lost and the hilt being sold separately in 1895.

It was inscribed: "The Captains of the Squadron under the Orders of Rear-Admiral Sir Horatio Nelson, K.B., desirous of testifying the high sense they entertain of his prompt decision and intrepid conduct in the attack of the French Fleet in Bequier Road off the Nile, the 1st of August, 1798, request his acceptance of a sword, and as a farther proof of thier (sic) esteem and regard, hope that he will permit his portrait to be taken and hung up in the room belonging to the Egyptian Club now established in commemoration of that glorious day.

Dated on board of His Majesty's ship *Orion* this 3rd of Aug. 1798, Jas. Saumarez, T. Troubridge, H. D. Darby, Thos. Louis, I. Peyton, Alexr. Jno. Ball, Saml. Hood, D. Gould, Th. Foley, R. Willett Miller, Ben Hallowell, E. Berry, T. M. Hardy." There is also inscribed on the guard: "Rear-Admiral Lord Nelson, Captain Sir E. Berry (*Vanguard*), Captain T. Troubridge (*Culloden*), Captain R. W. Miller (*Theseus*), Captain Alexr. J. Ball (*Alexander*) Captain Thos. Louis (*Minotaur*), Captain Sir T. B. Thompson (*Leander*) Captain B. Hallowell (*Swiftsure*) Captain Davidge Gould (*Audacious*) Captain John Peyton (*Defence*) Captain Sir Jas. Saumarez (*Orion*) Captain Thos. Foley (*Goliath*), Captain G. B. Westcott (*Majestic*), Captain H.D.E. Darby (*Bellerophon*), Captain T. M. Hardy (*Mutine*), Captain Saml. Hood (*Zealous*).

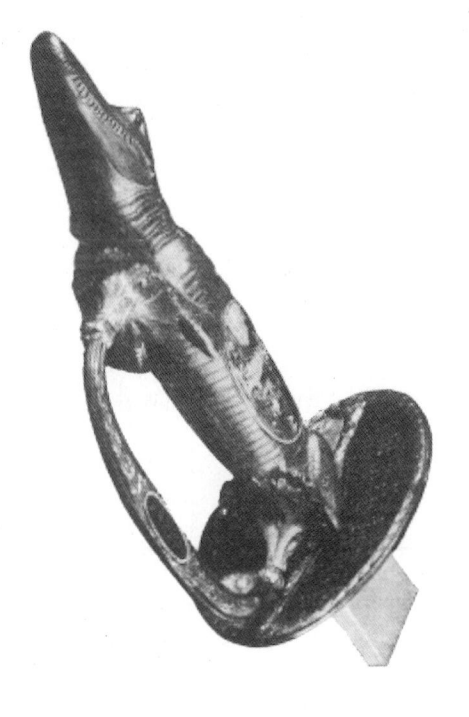

THE CHELENGK

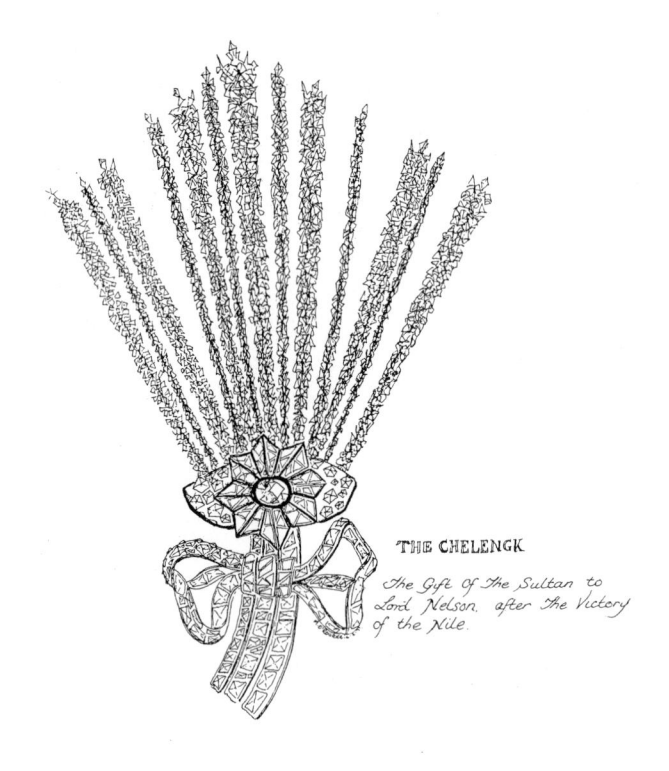

The Gift of the Sultan to Lord Nelson after the Victory of the Nile.

Chelengk

The tribute from the Sultan of Turkey, being ostentatious, appealed to Nelson's vanity, and consisted of a 'Plume of Triumph' made in diamonds. Comprising a central rose of flower of 16 petals with leaves and buds on either side, with, below it, a flower and true love knot to bind the spray together. Above it seven rays (later increased to 13 to represent the number of French ships taken or destroyed) shook or vibrated as the wearer moved. In due time the *Chelengk* was sold, being bought by Eyre-Matcham. Later it was bought by the Society of Nautical Research and presented to the National Art Collections Fund but was stolen in 1951. The thief later confessed having broken it up for disposal of the diamonds. (Copies are now sold by the National Maritime Museum)

'Duke of Bronté'

King Ferdinand created Nelson the Duke of Bronté, based on a 30,000-acre estate on the slopes of Mount Etna which, despite the grandeur of the title, proved to be of little practical value having being desolate and unproductive for years. Nonetheless the title 'Nelson and Bronté' proved appealing to Nelson and added to his satisfaction but further distinguished him from his colleagues.

The City of London presented him with a sword of honour worth two hundred guineas; The East India

Company a gift of £10,000; The Emperor of Russia a gold box set with diamonds; The King of Naples the sword with which Charles III of Spain had conquered Naples, and from the King of Sardinia a box set with diamonds.

In the House of Lords, Lord Minto said, 'In him, I have witnessed a degree of ability, judgment, temper and conciliation, not always allied to the sort of spirit which, without an instant's hesitation, can attack on one day the whole Spanish line with his single ship, and on another a superior French fleet, moored and fortified within the islands and shoals of an unknown Bay.'

His friends added to the joy – showering him with congratulations: St Vincent wrote exulting that his judgment of Nelson had been proved correct; Hood praised his victory as 'the most complete and splendid in History'; Collingwood could not express his joy at 'the complete and glorious victory.'

Other tributes were lavished on the conquering hero and the event of course prompted entrepreneurs to seek to catch the public mood and produce commemoratives in a variety of forms.

CHAPTER 7

'TREASURES' ON BOARD *L'ORIENT*

The extent of the looting of treasures by Napoleon during his one week stay on Malta in 1798 is well recorded and many authorities have written that these were lost together with a large amount of bullion, taken from Switzerland and Italy, when the *L'Orient* exploded late in the evening of the 1st August 1798. In his article on 'The Malta Treasure' (*The Nelson Dispatch* Vol 5 Part 8) Brian Tarpey pointed out that the generally held belief that the ship took the Malta Treasures with her to the bottom is not accurate:

'Nearly two months after the sinking of the *L'Orient* an account was sent on the 21st September 1798 from Cairo by the French Paymaster-General of Forces, General Esteve, to the National Treasury in France, in which he gave details of the Malta Treasure. Unfortunately, details of the merchants who bought parts of the treasure are not known, but the brief outlines contained in the account show that some silverware was left in Malta, various other silver objects were sold at Alexandria, diamonds and pearls and other jewels were sold by auction in Cairo, and other gold objects were converted into specie (coins) at the Mint of Cairo.'

Other treasure removed from Malta was captured at sea and taken to England but most were lost by fire although a cannon and a banner can be seen in the Tower of London and a sword is in the Louvre. Brian Tarpey's article concluded: - 'Finally, from 1983 to 1986 French divers salvaged relics from the ship and not only found the helm intact but discovered cannons, French silver coins, and other French objects. But not one piece of the Malta Treasure was found - it had been used for the purpose it had been looted - to pay for the upkeep of the French soldiers in Egypt.

Bronze rudder support stamped "No.6 Le Dauphin Royale" The original name of the French flagship L'Orient. Salved in Aboukir Bay

CHAPTER 8

COMMEMORATIVES AND CONTEMPORARY PRINTS

The rejoicing at the victory inevitably inspired painters, printers, medal and pottery manufacturers and others to commemorate the event.

Medals
"Nelson Commemorative Medals" by Thomas A. Hardy, published by *The Nelson Society* in 1985, lists no fewer than fourteen separate medals.

The Alexander Davison Medal
Alexander Davison, Nelson's Prize Agent and friend since his early days in Canada, produced at his expense the medal in gold for Admirals and Captains and in metals of declining value reflecting rank and these were issued to all taking part in the action. It was Davison who had dissuaded Nelson from abandoning his naval career in favour of the young and attractive Mary Simpson in Canada, to the national advantage.

Medal struck by Alexander Davison, engraved by P Roberts,
pub. August 1st. 1799 by Harrison, Cluse & Co No. 78 Fleet Street.

111

The Hancock/Kempson Medal, not issued until 1814, depicts a bust of Nelson (obv) and, on the reverse, the River God Nilus reclining left and viewing the action in the Bay. Captain Berry and Admiral Nelson.

Naval General Service Medal

The delay in the issue of the Naval General Service Medal until 1848 meant that only a small proportion of the *Vanguard* crew (as shown on the muster list) were alive to claim their entitlement. Amongst the applications for the medal it is reported that two females claimed - one in respect of the Battle of the Nile and the other the Battle of Trafalgar. Apparently the applications from the women received support from naval personnel but were overruled by the politicians who carried the day, and the medals were not awarded.

A late 18th Century small Prattware jug. Felix Pratt (1780-1859) gave his name to Prattware, distinctive earthenware in orange, blue, green and yellow. Relief jugs, manufactured for some thirty years in Staffordshire from the end of the eighteenth century, were popular and the opportunity was taken to combine the names of Nelson and Berry to mark the battle. Production of Commemorative Ware continues and Danbury Mint have recently produced a Battle of the Nile Tankard by Melvin Buckley as part of a collection of Horatio Nelson Tankards.

Pictures
The explosion of the *L'Orient* dominates many pictures and this awesome event stilled the battle for a while and the scene is depicted on our cover.

Literary field
Many eminent authors have covered the subject of the Battle and more will be published. Any student of the battle could well start a trail by reading *The Dispatches and Letters of Vice Admiral Lord Viscount Nelson* with notes by Sir Nicholas Harris Nicolas GCMG. now available in paperback (ISBN 1-86 176-049-3).

CONTEMPORARY PRINTS
FROM THE
DORMERS COLLECTION

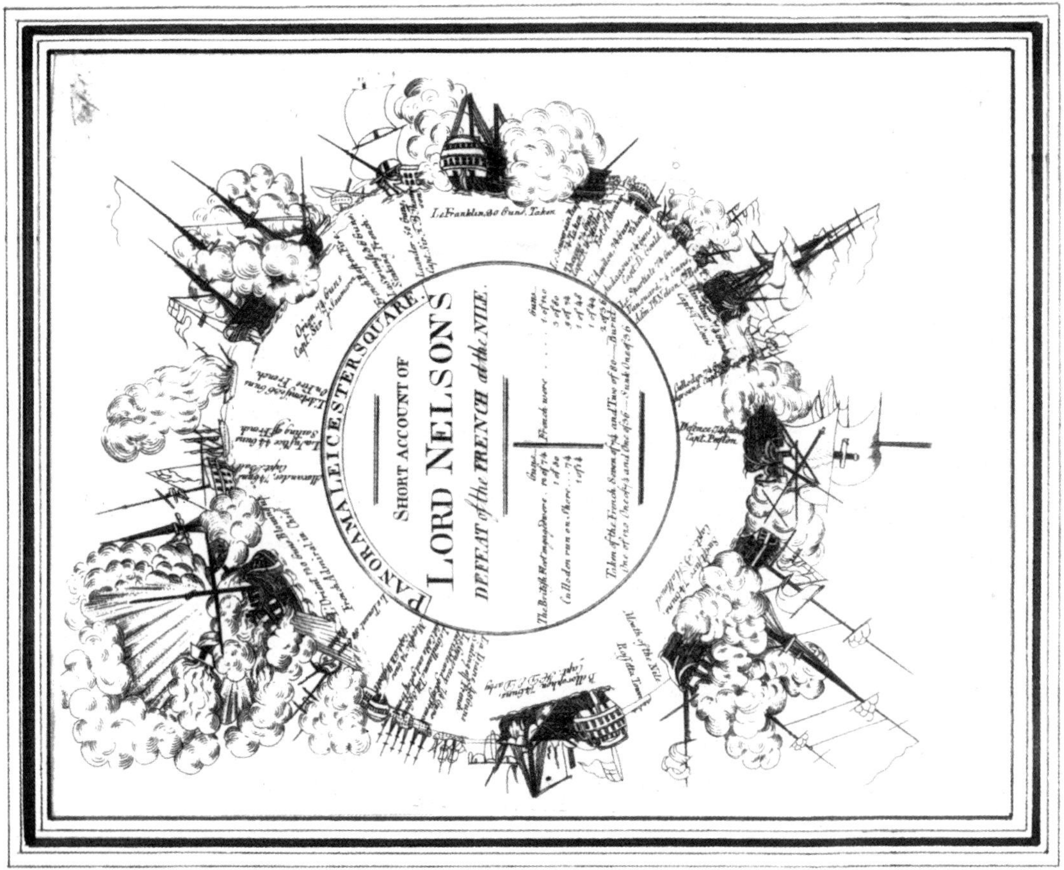
PANORAMA LEICESTER SQUARE.
SHORT ACCOUNT OF
LORD NELSON'S
DEFEAT of the FRENCH at the NILE.

LORD NELSON

From the portrait recently presented to the National Portrait Gallery

The original portrait of Lord Nelson was painted for him by Leonardo Guzzardi, of Palermo, in 1799. Nelson is shown wearing the aigrette, consisting of an artificial plume, covered with pearls, which was given to him by the Grand Seignior Selim III after the Battle of the Nile, and the portrait was presented by Lord Nelson to the Sultan in return for the latter's gift. It is a copy of this picture which the Sultan has just presented to the National Portrait Gallery.

116

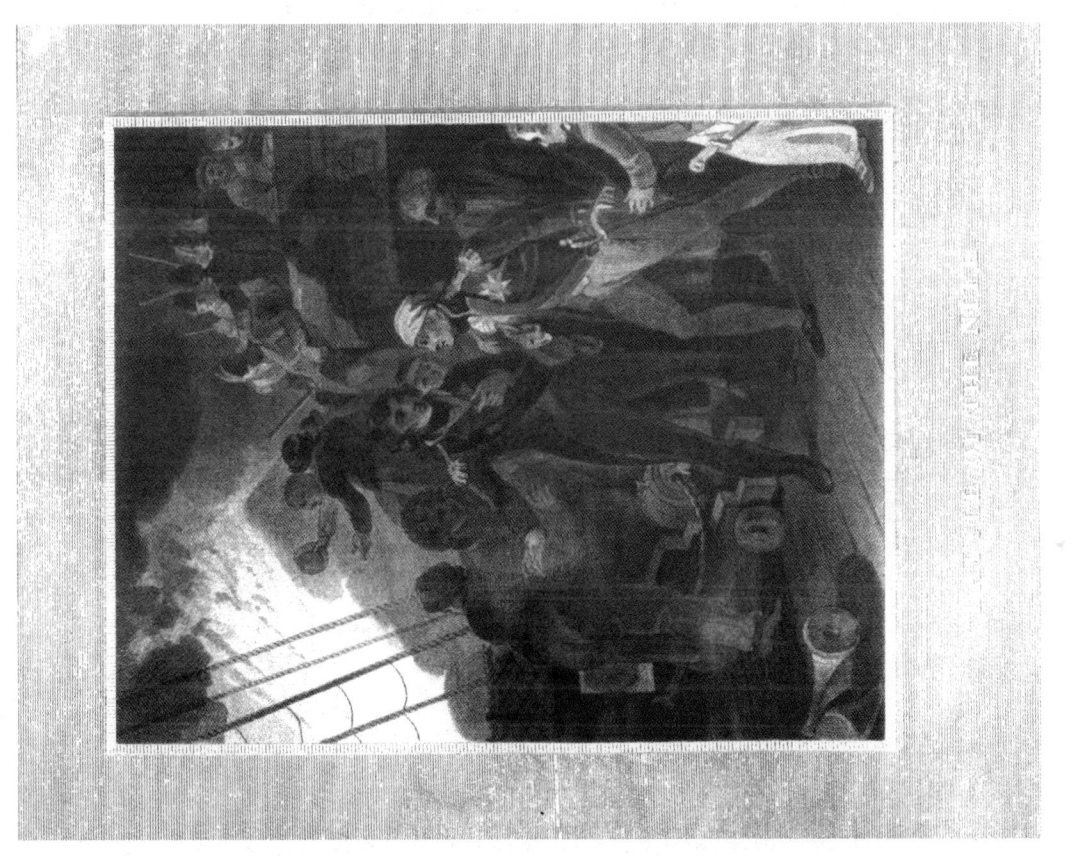

BATTLE OF THE NILE

W. Bromley del. W. H Worthington sculp.

Published by R. Bowyer, Pall Mall, London. March 1, 1801

THE BATTLE OF THE NILE
AUGUST 1 1798

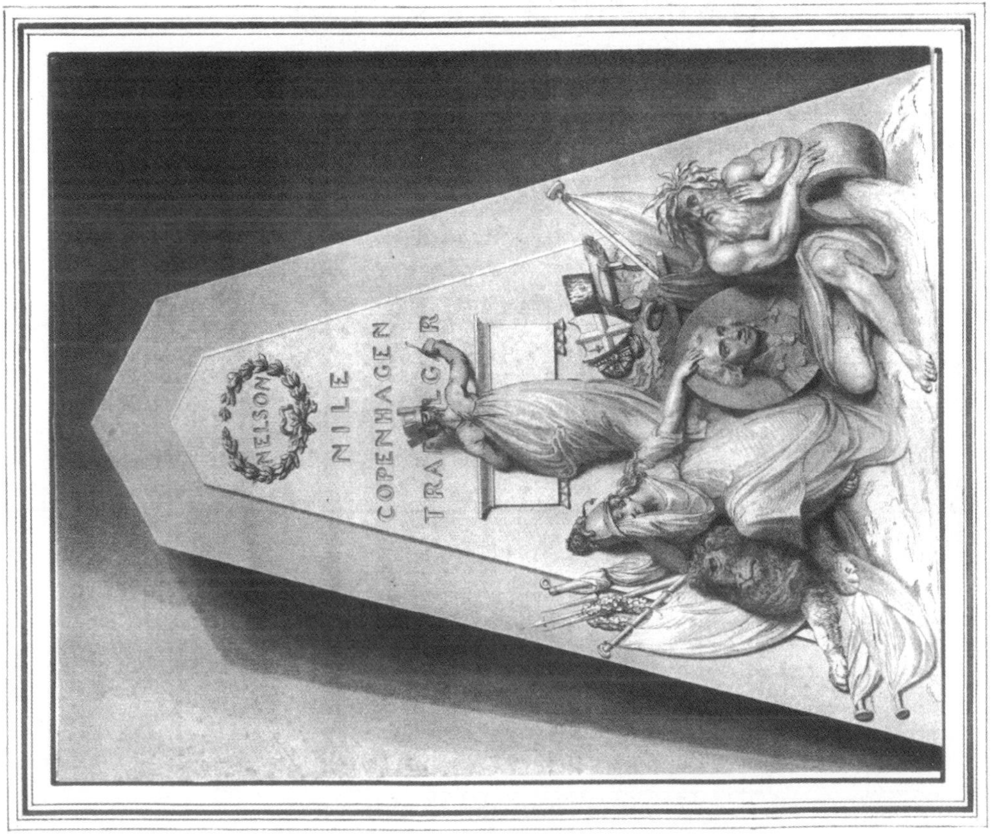
NELSON
NILE
COPENHAGEN

CHAPTER 9

BIOGRAPHICAL NOTES

THOMAS ALLEN*
MICHAEL AUSTIN*
EDWARD BERRY
THOMAS BLADEN CAPEL
WALES CLODD
HENRY COMPTON
STEPHEN GEORGE COMYN
WILLIAM FADDY
EDWARD GALWAY
JOSIAH NISBET
NATHANIEL VASSALL
JAMES WESTICOTT
JOHN WATHERSTON

*Listed in *Nelson's Heroes* by Graham Dean and Keith Evans
Published by *The Nelson Society* 1994 ISBN 0 95 10702 5 8

Thomas ALLEN

Thomas Allen was born in the village of Sculthorpe, near Burnham Thorpe, Norfolk, in the year 1771. From the earliest years, Thomas was in the service of the Nelson family, and when Horatio took command of the *Agamemnon* (64), Tom Allen, with others from the area went along with the captain to start his career in the Royal Navy. On board the *Agamemnon*, Tom was promoted after some daring deed to replace Frank Lepeé as Nelson's servant and accompanied him at all times. During the action he would be stationed at one of the upper deck guns close to his master; on more than one occasion, when under fire, he interposed his bulky form to shield the much smaller Nelson. He fought at Nelson's side in the glorious boarding action at St. Vincent and received a severe wound in doing so.

Tom Allen was in charge of Nelson's personal effects, his jewels, plate, valuables, and all things belonging to him on board. He also acted as body servant, and as such, he often had to coax his little master from a wet deck and a raging storm. It has been said that he was too familiar with Nelson: on one occasion he told him off, in front of other officers, for taking an extra glass of wine, by saying, "no more now, you know it will only make you ill."

Tom was for some time at Nelson's home, Merton Place, but he did not go with the hero to Trafalgar; who knows, if he had, perhaps Nelson would have survived the battle. A few years after Nelson's death, Tom volunteered again for the Navy serving off the coast of Spain on the *Circe,* He returned to Burnham, becoming manservant to Sir William Bolton another "old Agamemnon" and Nelson's relative. Sir William's death left Tom in penury, but he was saved by the intervention of Sir Thomas Hardy, who was then Governor of Greenwich Hospital. Hardy appointed him pewterer to the Hospital, and it was from this comfortable situation he was called by a very sudden death. He is buried in the old cemetery, Greenwich, close to the grave of Captain Hardy. There is a fine memorial to him still standing above his grave and the inscription is as follows:-

Litho from Tom Allen's obituary to The Mirror of Literature, Amusement and Instruction, 9.11.1839
Courtesy Adrian Bridge

**To the Memory
of
Thomas Allen
The Faithful Servant
of
Admiral Lord Nelson
Born at
Burnham Thorpe
in the
County of Norfolk
1764
and died at
the Royal Hospital
Greenwich
on the
23rd November
1838**

*Tom (seated right) holds Nelson's portrait
from Greenwich Pensioners on Trafalgar Day 1835
National Maritime Museum, London.*

123

Michael AUSTIN (1772-1844)

Michael Austin first comes to light at the Glorious 1st of June, where he served under Admiral Howe. He next appears as Nelson's boatswain in his flagship *Vanguard* at the Battle of the Nile, where he lost an arm in the action. After spending his later years at Her Majesty's Dockyard, Chatham, Michael Austin died at his residence, Nile Cottage, Gillingham, near Chatham, Kent on June 1st 1844, aged 72. He was buried in a vault in the churchyard of St Mary Magdelene, Gillingham, Kent on June 7th 1844 and a memorial was placed in the church by his son, Horatio Thomas Austin.

The Reverend Canon Peter Absolon who helped discover Michael Austin has kindly given the following interesting family information:

> My great-grandmother, Maria Chambers, (nee Damant) who lived in Colkirk, Norfolk and was born in 1822, used to play with the children of Mrs Girdlestone, Lord Nelson's niece, who was sister to Lady Bolton and sister also of the 3rd Lord Nelson. Maria Damant took a lead in the charades, plays and dances at the Boltons' home at Burnham, which was crammed with relics and possessions of Nelson.
>
> Lady Bolton allowed Maria to rummage among the contents of the row of chests in the long roomy attic. She said, when she was an old woman, 'Many a time I have dressed up in his uniforms and his cocked hat too. Yes, and I have run about the house brandishing his sword and thought nothing of it.' One of Nelson's great-nephews loved my great-grandmother long and hopelessly (her father would not give his consent) and he went abroad. When he came home from South Africa as an old man he visited her in Norfolk and they talked day after day of the old times they shared. Some of the Damants, however, did intermarry with the Girdlestons so I suppose I can almost qualify as a relic of Nelson!

There are two inscriptions relating to Michael Austin. The first, on the vault in the churchyard of St Mary Magdelene in Gillingham, Kent, reads:

Sacred
to the memory of
Thomas Fitzherbert Austin,
Son of
Michael & Mary Austin,
who departed this life, 28th June 1825,
aged 14 years
Also John William Rawlinson, son of
the Revd. John Samuel Rawlinson, decd.
21st of August 1826, Aged 11 months and 13 days.
Jane Fitzherbert Austin,
Daughter of the above
Michael and Mary Ann Austin,
Mother of the above Thomas and Jane,
Died on the 10th September 1829
Aged 51 years.
Also of George Daysh Austin,
Assistant Surgeon of H.M. Mary and member of
the Royal College of Surgeons, Lond,
son of the above
Michael and Mary Ann Austin,
who died 6th June 1836, aged 27 years.
Also of Mr. Michael Austin
who died 1st June 1844, aged 72 years.

The second, inside the church, is a white marble tablet, in the form of a shield, bordered by plain black marble. It is situated on the north wall of arches close to the great cross arch, and immediately below the tablet of Neil Sloman Esq. It reads:

> In memory of
> Michael Austin,
> who died June 1st 1844
> Aetat 72,
> And of Mary Anne, his Wife
> who died September 10th 1829
> Aetat 51.
> Their remains are interred
> in this churchyard.
> This tablet is erected
> As a mark of respect and affection
> by their Son,
> Horatio Thomas Austin,
> The only survivor
> of eight children.

Sir Edward BERRY (1768-1831)

Sir Edward Berry was one of a large family left in straitened circumstances by the early death of his father, a merchant in London. Through Lord Mulgrave, the boy was, in 1779, appointed as a volunteer to the *Burford,* 70 guns, with Captain Rainier, then sailing for the East Indies, where she remained till after the conclusion of the war in 1783. He was made lieutenant on 20 January 1794, as a reward it is said, for his gallantry in boarding a French ship of war. He is said also to have distinguished himself on the First of June; but the first distinct mention of him is on his appointment to the *Agamemnon* with Captain Nelson in May 1796. He quickly won Nelson's esteem (*Nelson Dispatches*, ii. 175), followed him in the Captain (11 June), and whilst Nelson was on shore conducting the siege of Porto Ferrajo, Berry, commanded the ship in such a manner as to call forth an official expression of his captain's 'fullest approbation'. The role of Captain Berry in the Battle of the Nile is outlined in the summary of the action. Nelson ordered Flag Captin Berry to carry home his dispatches on the *Leander*, Captain Thompson. The *Leander* had the misfortune to fall in with one of the ships which had escaped from Aboukir, The *Gènèreux*, 80 gun (936) men off Crete. In the ensuing unequal battle with *Leander,*50 gun (282) men severe damage and casualties were sustained and, with the agreement of Captain Berry,the *Leander* surrendered.

Rough treatment was meted out to the prisoners but this was eventually relieved by an exchange of prisoners and Captain Berry was to arrive in London in December to a hero's welcome. Knighted on the 12th December, 1798 he was presented with the freedom of the City. Early in the spring of 1799 he was appointed to the *Foudroyant*, and directed to assist in the blockade of Malta. In this role Berry had the gratification of assisting in the capture of his former captor, the *Génèreux* on the 18th February and the *Guillaume Tell* on 31 March, the last of the French ships which had been at the Battle of the Nile. The following June the *Foudroyant* carried the Queen of Naples from Palermo to Leghorn but a few months later he returned to England. In the summer of 1805 he was appointed to the *Agamemnon* and was present at Trafalgar but had no opportunity for special distinction. In 1806 he as made baronet and, after further service, in 1813 he was placed in charge of one of the royal yachts. Appointed rear-admiral in 1821 he never hoisted his flag, being in poor health and died on 13 February 1831 without issue - the baronetcy becoming extinct.

128

Published by G. Riley, Jan 20, 1798 *Warwick Leadlay Gallery*

Action between HMS Leander (50 guns and 282 men) and the French National Ship Le Généreux (74 guns and 936 men) August 18, 1798, the Leander raking the Le Généreux. C.H. Seaforth, Artist and Engraver. National Maritime Museum, London.

Hon Sir Thomas Bladen CAPEL CB GCB (1776-1853)

The Honourable Thomas Capel entered the navy in 1792 aged 16 and in the following year became a midshipman in which capacity he served in *Sanspareil* (80) in Lord Bridport's action off l'Orient in 1795. He became a lieutenant in 1797 and was *Vanguard's* signal officer at the Battle of the Nile; after the battle Nelson entrusted him with a duplicate set of dispatches reporting the defeat of the French fleet.

The original set sent via the *Leander* (50) was however lost when she was captured. Fortunately Lieutenant Capel successfully delivered his dispatches and was confirmed in the rank of commander on the 2 October 1798. Less than three months later he was a captain and commanded a number of ships – mostly frigates. In 1802 he was appointed to command another frigate, the *Phoebe* (36) and in this ship he was present at the ultimate sea battle of the time – Trafalgar.

Captain Capel distinguished himself in the aftermath of the battle by saving the French *Swiftsure* (74) and by helping to capture the Spanish *Bahama* (74). He sat on the court-martial of Sir Robert Calder and was with Duckworth in the Dardenelles in 1807. After many more years at sea he achieved flag-rank in 1825 and was Commander-in-Chief at Portsmouth in 1848. He died in London in 1853 having received three clasps to his Naval General Service medal.

Wales CLODD

Wales Clodd's duties as *Vanguard's* Master during the expedition in search of the French fleet included keeping a log . This log was first published by the Navy Records Society in 1900 and contains valuable information about the movements of the flagship, the sighting of the enemy, the battle itself and the aftermath. Unfortunately nothing further is known at the present of Wales Clodd or his career.

Henry COMPTON (1774-1847)

Henry Compton was a native of Limerick, born in 1774 and received the naval part of his education at an academy near Deptford. He joined the navy as a midshipman in January 1789 on board the *Cumberland* (74) and first sent to sea in the *Actæon* (44) conveying troops to and from the West Indies. On the breaking out of the French Revolutionary War, he joined the *Romulus* (36) in time to witness the occupation to Toulon. He next served with the Channel fleet on board the *Minotaur* (74), and subsequently returned to the Mediterranean, in the *Blonde* (32).

Early in 1795 he transferred in *Britannia* (100) then *Victory* (100), flagships of Vice-Admiral Hotham and Sir John Jervis. It was probably through the latter connection that he came to the attention of Nelson. In March 1796 Compton was promoted to lieutenant having been drafted into *Agamemnon* (64) two months earlier.

Thereafter he served with Nelson for three dramatic years seeing action in the Mediterranean, the Battle of Cape St. Vincent, at Tenerife and finally at the Battle of the Nile where he served in *Vanguard*. A year after the Nile, Nelson shifted his flag into *Foudroyant* (80) and directed Compton to take command of the *Perseus* bomb vessel. A letter from Nelson to the Admiralty written on the first anniversary of the Nile commended Compton "I beg leave to recommend [him] as highly meriting promotion." He married, in 1807, Miss Molloy, niece to Edward Molloy, of Oporto, and had issue four sons and one daughter. Commander Compton commanded ships at the blockades of Alexandria and Malta, and along the Italian coast. In 1840 he accepted the rank of Captain and died in 1847.

Stephen George COMYN (1766-1839)

The Rev. Stephen Comyn, Nelson's chaplain at the Nile, 1798 in The Vanguard
Mrs D.M.V. Hurst

Born in 1766, Stephen Comyn gained his B.A. in 1788 and at the age of 32 entered the *Vanguard* (74) as Nelson's chaplain on 31 March 1798. Not every ship in the Navy employed a chaplain, the seamen in their superstitious way being wary of them and many chaplains found themselves teaching the young midship-men their three R's as well as administering the faith. Nelson seems to have had his share of clergy including his brother William in the *Boreas*, his cousin, Robert Rolfe, *Agamemnon* and finally Alexander John Scott in the *Victory*, whose duties included linguist and secretary to the Admiral. There was possibly a family con-nection between Comyn and Scott as Comyn's surname was the same as Scott's mother's maiden name.

During the Battle of the Nile Comyn was summoned, at the height of the conflict, to find Nelson bloodied from a head wound and convinced he wasn't long for this world but the surgeon soon assured him all was well. Following the great victory Nelson issued a memorandum to his fleet, "Almighty God having blessed His Majesty's arms with victory, the Admiral intends returning public thanksgiving for the same at 2 o'clock this day and he recommends every ship doing the same as soon as convenient."

The Reverend Comyn conducted the service from the quarterdeck of the *Vanguard* which greatly impressed a group of captured French officers. On 8 June, 1799 Comyn, in company with Hardy and the lieutenants of the *Vanguard*, joined Nelson in his new flagship *Foudroyant* (80) where they languished 'inactive at a foreign court'. One can only guess what Comyn thought of Nelson's behaviour at Naples during a period which even the most ardent of Nelson supporters have regarded as slightly decadent. Christmas Eve, 1800, Comyn transferred to *San Josef* (112) Nelson's old prize from the Battle of St. Vincent. The Spring of 1801 found the British Fleet in the Baltic for the attack on the Danes at Copenhagen where Comyn now became chaplain of Nelson's ship, the *St. George* (98). As the *St. George* was too large for Nelson's needs in the shallow waters off Copenhagen he transferred to the *Elephant* (74); whether Comyn removed with him for the day is uncertain but now the chaplain was reaching the end of his service with the Navy and he approached Nelson with a request for a living ashore. Having heard nothing by October 1801, he wrote to remind Nelson of his offer to help. Nelson told him to be patient: "I never have forgot you that is not my disposition."*

In June 1802 Nelson was able to write the following to Comyn:- "My dear Sir, I send you the Chancellor's letter, and most sincerely congratulate you on your preferment, which to a person who has conducted himself so prudently in pecuniary affairs will make you truly comfortable."

Horatio N.W. Comyn followed his father into the Church and was Rector of Brunstead (The more modern spelling is Brumstead) and Walcott in Norfolk until his death in 1887.

It is to our former Chairman, Ron Fiske, that we are indebted for the description of the Comyn arms and crest illustrated:

> "Azure a chevron ermine between three garbs of cumin or. Crest: two arms embowed proper couped at the shoulders habited ermine holding in the hands a garb of cumin or"

[*Nelson to Comyn, 8 October, 1801. *Ben Burgess Nelson Memorabilia Collection*.]

For a deeper understanding of the terms used in heraldry and of the Nelson Heraldry readers are recommended to consult *Nelson and Associated Heraldry - A guide* by R.C.Fiske, published by The Nelson Society in 1983.

Stephen Comyn had two sons by his wife, Charlotte: the first, George Robert, joined the Royal Navy and died in 1816, the second he named after his Admiral, Horatio Nelson William Comyn. The preferment mentioned was St. Mary the Virgin, Bridgham, Norfolk, where the Reverend Comyn was to serve for the remaining 36 years of his life. He died on the 17th March 1839 at the age of 73 and was buried near the altar of St. Mary's. A memorial to him reads:-

Sacred
To the memory of the
Reverend Stephen George Comyn
36 years Rector of this Parish
who died
17th of March 1839
Aged 73 years
Chaplain to Vice Admiral Lord Nelson
Was with him in the Battle of the Nile
And at Copenhagen
And was presented to the Rectory of this Parish
By the Chancellor through the intercession of Lord Nelson
During the space of 36 years he enjoyed an
Unremitted state of good health till the last
Fortnight when it pleased the Almighty to afflict
Him with severe sufferings, which be bore with
Great resignation, and may
His soul rest in peace in hopes of joyful Resurrection.

William FADDY (... -1798)

Little has been discovered to date of Captain of Marines, William Faddy killed in *Vanguard* at the Battle of the Nile. It is recorded that Nelson wrote of him as follows: -

"To John Locker St. Helens 8th April 1798
Captain Faddy is embarked in the Ship, and assure your good father of my attention to whoever he recommends. Captain Faddy appears a very good kind of man. Captain Berry has taken his son on board.
HORATIO NELSON"

Given the presence on board of his son, his death was all the more poignant. After his death, Nelson sought the assistance of Earl Spencer, writing: -

"Vanguard, at Sea 19thSept 1798
Captain Faddy, of the Marines who was killed on board the *Vanguard* has a family of small children: the eldest son is now on board this Ship, only fourteen years of age. I beg to solicit your Lordship for a Commission in the Marines for him. I understand it has been done and the youth permitted to remain at school, till of a proper age to join the Corps. If, however, this should, in the present instance, be thought wrong, may I request that his name may stand as an élève of the Admiralty, and Mrs Faddy acquainted with it, which must give her some relief under her great misfortune.
Ever your Lordship's most obedient Servant, HORATIO NELSON"

Years later Nelson visited Captain Faddy's widow and presented her with his own Nile Gold Medal. William Faddy junior served in the *Victory* as a lieutenant in 1804, but he also died in the service of his country in 1811.

Edward GALWAY* (???-1844)

This officer became a lieutenant in June 1793; he served for a short time as *Vanguard*'s first lieutenant in which time the Battle of the Nile took place. Lieutenant Galway played an active part in the battle. Two hours after *Vanguard* began an exchange of gunfire with the French *Spartiate* (74) the enemy ship struck her colours. Lieutenant Galway and a party of marines were sent to take possession of her which he successfully achieved. Spartiate was in time added to the British fleet and fought seven years later at Trafalgar. In recognition of Galway's contribution to the victory over the French, Nelson promoted him to Commander in October, 1798. He was promoted to Captain in 1802 and was present in *Dryad* (36) at the Scheldt expedition in 1809. Five years later (still commanding *Dryad*) Captain Gallway further distinguished himself in the capture of the French *Clorinde* (40). He gained flag rank in 1837 and died in 1844 as a Rear-Admiral of the Red.

*Spellings vary. This ship's muster list has him as Galway (to which we defer on this occasion), as does the *Commissioned Sea Officers* (Syrett & DiNardi) but the *Vanguard*'s Master's log, the *Naval History of Great Britain* (James) and *Dispatches of Lord Nelson* (Nicolas) each have him as Galwey.

Josiah NISBET (1780-1830)
Stepson of Lord Nelson

Josiah Nisbet was entered and appeared on the Muster List from the 15th August, 1798. Frances Nisbet, later to become Lady Nelson, had returned to Nevis with her infant son Josiah after the death in Salisbury of her husband Dr. Josiah Nisbet. In Nevis she was to manage the household of the President of Nevis, her uncle, Mr. Herbert and it was he who would find, to his amazement, Nelson playing on all fours under the dining room table with the young Josiah during a visit.

Married in 1787 Nelson, Frances and the young Josiah returned to England for the 'five years on the beach' although Josiah attended a boarding school arranged by the Revd. William Nelson.

On Nelson's appointment to the *Agamemnon* in January 1793 Josiah joined him as a Midshipman and his subsequent meteoric rise in the Navy was not entirely due to patronage but to ability and demonstrated courage. With Nelson at the Battle of Cape St. Vincent he was a Lieutenant of the *Theseus* at the time of the failed Santa Cruz expedition but he was instrumental in saving his stepfather's life when he applied a tourniquet to the shattered right arm.

In the Mediterranean in 1797 he was Captain of the *Dolphin* (24) (hospital ship) and *La Bonne Citoyenne* (20) a captured sloop with a complement of 120, and *Buona Ventura* (hired brig). Josiah arrived at Aboukir Bay on the 15th August, 1798, on the same day the *Mutine* sailed carrying Nelson's dispatch to Naples. He had been sent by St. Vincent with a message for Nelson to return to Minorca if he had not made contact with the French fleet. He also carried a sealed letter for Nelson from the Commander-in-Chief to the effect that whilst he had met Nelson's request regarding his son-in-law. "It would be a breach of friendship to conceal from you that he loves drink and low company, is thoroughly ignorant of all forms of service, inattentive, obstinate, and wrongheaded beyond measure, and had he not been your son-in-law must have been annihilated months ago. With all this, he is honest and truth-telling, and, I dare say, will, if you ask him, subscribe to every word I have written." After two weeks exhilarating activity with his 'band of brothers' the letter must have come as a great shock and hurt Nelson deeply.

Interpretations of the meeting of the President of Nevis with Nelson playing with the young Josiah

1) From Southey's *Life of Nelson* (Henry Bohn's edition 1861, Bell & Daldy editions 1866 and 1870 Greage Bell and Sons 1881 and 1989)

2) From the *Life and Naval Memoirs*
3) *of Lord Nelson*
(Pub: Willoughby & Co., Glasgow)

3) The marriage in Nevis

138

Later Josiah sailed in the *Buona Ventura* to Naples and joined in the festivities orchestrated by the Ambassador's wife, Lady Hamilton. Josiah had met the Hamiltons in 1793 but he was to be affected by Emma's charms and to be well aware of the effect she was having on Nelson. In his cups he vented his feelings and relations between stepfather and son became strained. Nevertheless he was given command of the frigate *Thalia* (36) and sent on various missions but news of his unsatisfactory conduct became known. *Thalia* was ordered back to Portsmouth for a refit and was paid off on arrival in 1800. Nelson was to recommend to the Admiralty that he should not be given another ship and this terminated Josiah's naval career.

Ashore he partook of the fast life for a while but eventually settled with his mother in Exmouth. His joy there was his ownership of a gaff rigged yacht, an interest shared with Frances Evans, who became his wife at Littleham Church on the 31st March 1819. Subsequently he moved to Paris, became a successful dealer in Government Stocks and Bonds, and was joined by Lady Nelson. A chill, which turned to pleurisy, proved fatal and he died aged fifty. A tomb was arranged in Littleham, which contains his body, and family members and it is there that Lady Nelson lies.

Richard Kerr-Nesbitt in his monograph published by the Nesbitt/Nisbet Society summed up his career in the following words:- "Josiah did not achieve fame, but he certainly lived an eventful life to the full. He sailed 'close to the wind'- often lived dangerously."

His continuing loyalty to his mother must have been a source of strength to her.

William Standway PARKINSON (????-1838)

William Standway Parkinson gained his lieutenancy in May 1794 and served as a junior Lieutenant of the *Dido* (28), in her gallant action with *La Minerve*, French frigate, 24 June 1795. He served with Nelson in *Vanguard* at the Battle of the Nile in 1798. He transferred with Nelson into *Foudroyant* (80) whilst in Naples following the battle and was for a while the ship's first lieutenant. It was during this period that the Caraccioli affair arose and Parkinson was fortunate enough not to have been court-martialled himself. Lieutenant Parkinson was given charge of Caraccioli before his court-martial and execution. According to James (*Naval History of Great Britain*,

1860 edition) Parkinson was asked to intercede with Nelson on Caraccioli's behalf as the latter feared hanging. Nelson in no uncertain terms informed Parkinson that the prisoner had been "fairly tried by the officers of his own country; I cannot interfere". On being urged a second time by Lieutenant Parkinson, [Nelson] exclaimed with much agitation, "Go, Sir, and attend to your duty!" Carraccioli then, as a last hope asked Lieutenant Parkinson whether he thought an application to Lady Hamilton would prove beneficial. Upon which that officer went to the quarter-deck, but, not being able to meet with her, he returned."

As history records, Caraccioli was duly hung as a traitor to the Kingdom of Naples within hours. Despite this episode and given Parkinson's obvious feelings, it did not seem to have damaged his career. Nelson sent him home two weeks later with his dispatches and a letter of commendation: 'I beg leave to recommend Lieutenant Parkinson.' Promotion to Commander followed a few weeks later (October 1799) on his arrival in London. He married, in 1800, the only daughter of the Rev. Edward Clarke, of Uckfield, Sussex. He became a Captain in 1808 and died on 19 May 1838.

James WESTICOTT (or WESTCOTT)

John Westicott served as *Vanguard*'s Master-at-Arms during 1798 and five days after the Battle of the Nile he was promoted to Lieutenant. At present nothing more is known of this officer.

Nathaniel VASSALL (-1832)

Lieutenant Nathaniel Vassell gained his rank in 1790 and was appointed to the *Foudroyant* (80) as second lieutenant in January 1798. However by March we find him as second lieutenant in *Vanguard* (74) in which he served at the Battle of the Nile. During the battle Lieutenant Vassall was sent away with a boarding party of marines to take possession of a prize. He returned three and a half hours later with the news that the prize had got underway and escaped. Vassall was wounded at the battle but survived. He was made commander in 1814 and died in 1832.

John WATHERSTON (1771-1804)

Born in 1771 in Legerwood, Berwickshire, John was one of 10 children born to Peter and Katherine who farmed in the area. He joined the *Vanguard* (74) as Midshipman on the 19th February 1798 and six days later was classed as Master's Mate. Following the Battle of the Nile John continued in service but in the winter of 1804, as Lieutenant, was lost at sea. In the Kirkyard of Legerwood, Berwickshire, his family erected a headstone to his memory which reads:-

> This stone is placed here
> In memory of
> John
> Son of Peter Watherston
> Tenant of East Moriston
> A Lieutenant of His Majestyís Fleet
> Who
> With all other officers
> And crew of a man of war
> Perished in the Atlantic Ocean
> by the tempestuous weather
> about the end of 1804
> in the 33rd year of his age.

On the first of Aug. 1798 at the Battle of the Nile he served in the same ship and under the immediate eye and command of the great and gallant Nelson and from his conduct as an officer on the memorable occasion as well as in other times and days of trial, he gained the approbation and friendship and patronage of the immortal hero.

(*Footnote – on the muster list he is shown as Weatherstone*).

The Nelson Society – 1998

Founded 1981 – Registered Charity No: 296979

President
The Right Honourable the Earl Nelson

Life Vice-Presidents
Ben Burgess M.B.E. – Mrs Anna Tribe, O.B.E., J.P. – Clive Richards

Chairman
Derek HAYES
16 Silver Lane, Billingshurst, W Sussex RH14 9RJ Tel/Fax 01403 782496
Email: derek.hayes@which.net

Vice Chairman
David SHANNON
39 Woodland Mount, Hertford. Hertfordshire SG13 7JD Tel 01992 550443

Website: http://www.ean.co.uk/Great_Yarmouth/Clubs_Societies/Nelson/index.htm

The Nelson Dispatch

The purpose of **The Nelson Dispatch** is to further the aim of **The Nelson Society** which is to promote public education and appreciation of the character and life of Admiral Lord Nelson

The Nelson Society

LIST OF PUBLICATIONS

1983	*Nelson and Associated Heraldry – A Guide****	R.C. Fiske
1984	*Santa Cruz****	Michael Nash
1985	*Nelson Commemorative Medals 1797 – 1905*	Thomas A. Hardy
1987	*A catalogue of Picture Postcards*	David Shannon
1988	*The Men who fought with NELSON in HMS VICTORY at TRAFALGAR****	Charles Addis
1989	*A tour along the Norfolk/Suffolk Border in Nelson and Suckling Country****	Michael Nash
	Notices of Nelson extracted from Norfolk and Norwich Notes and Queries	R.C. Fiske
1990	*The Battle of Copenhagen Roads*	Captain F. Volke
1990	*Invincible 1765 – 1801*	Derek Hayes
1991	*A Brief Guide to Nelson and Bath****	Louis Hodgkin
1992	*A visit to Melford Hall, home of Sir Richard Hyde Parker, Bt.*	Derek Hayes
1994	*Nelson's Heroes*	Graham Dean & Keith Evans
	Nelson: The Sussex Tradition	David Shannon

Pamphlets

1997	*Admiral Lord Nelson*	Rona Dickinson
	Collecting Nelson Postcards	David Shannon
	Nelson's Last Walk	Colin White

*** Out of print

Copies, including back copies of **The Nelson Dispatch**, are available from: The Sales Manager, 16 Silver Lane, BILLINGHURST, West Sussex RH14 9RJ. Tel/Fax: 01403 782496.